THE BLACK HAND
AT SARAJEVO

Also by Henry Gilfond

THE REICHSTAG FIRE
HEROINES OF AMERICA
PLAYS FOR READING
JOURNEY WITHOUT END

THE BLACK HAND AT SARAJEVO 🐍🐍🐍
by Henry Gilfond

THE BOBBS-MERRILL COMPANY, INC.
Indianapolis / New York

ISBN 0–672–52070–2
Library of Congress catalog card number 74–17690
Designed by Paula Wiener
Manufactured in the United States of America

First printing

To my mother and father

Contents

Introduction, IX

1. Appointment in Sarajevo, 1
2. Assassination, 11
3. The Prussian Position, 27
4. Triple Entente, 35
5. Austria-Hungary and the Serbian Unrest, 43
6. The Secret Societies, 51
7. The Black Hand, 57
8. The Plot, 66
9. The Assassins Move to Sarajevo, 79
10. The Efforts to Stop the Assassins, 86
11. On the Eve of the Assassination, 93
12. The Political Murder, 98
13. Europe Reacts: The Norm and the Unexpected, 106
14. Investigation, 118
15. Ultimatum, 123
16. Mobilization, 132
17. War, 144
18. America Decided, 155
19. Trials and Judgment, 166

Introduction

THERE were some forty significant political murders in the first thirteen years of the twentieth century—of generals, prime ministers, kings, queens, princes, and presidents, including our own President William McKinley in the year 1901. There were many political murders in the nineteenth century, including the assassination of Abraham Lincoln in 1865. In recent years we have been witness to, and horrified by, the seemingly endless number of political murders of just ordinary people in Ireland; of innocent people at the airport in Athens; of Israeli athletes at the Olympic Games in Munich. In the United States we were stunned by the political assassination of President John F. Kennedy; of his brother, Senator Robert F. Kennedy; of the Nobel Peace Prize winner and leader of American blacks, Martin Luther King, Jr. Yet no political murder before or since equaled, for sheer dramatic, world-shaking consequence, the political assassinations perpetrated by the terrorist organization, the Black Hand, on the streets of Sarajevo, the capital of the small Austrian province of Bosnia, on the morning of June 28, 1914.

When Martin Luther King, Jr., was assassinated, there were street demonstrations and some riots; but they were of a local nature and soon died out. When

John F. Kennedy was assassinated, there was a bit of a
financial tremor on Wall Street; but Lyndon B. Johnson
assumed the presidency of the United States, and, except for the profound sorrow which lingered with the
nation, the murder of the American chief of state has
not seemed to cause any marked change in the course
of the world's history.

However, when Franz Ferdinand, the archduke of
Austria-Hungary, and his wife were gunned down on
the streets of Sarajevo by the Black Hand, June 28,
1914, all the capitals of the greater powers in Europe,
and of some of the minor powers, went into immediate,
feverish action. There were threats and counterthreats,
ultimatums; sabers rattled, armies were hurriedly
mobilized, guns and troops moved swiftly to their borders, and within five quick weeks all of Europe was
engaged in the bloodiest war of its history. It was a war
which eventually would involve almost all the nations
of the world, including the United States.

Franz Ferdinand was heir to the throne of the Austro-Hungarian Empire, but mightier men, more important men, had been assassinated before him, and have
been since, without creating any kind of major
upheaval. Actually, his murder was met with indifference, even relief, by many of the leading princes and
politicians of his own country, as well as by government
officials and political observers in other European capitals.

As a matter of fact, there were many who believed
at that time, and even today, that the assassination of
the archduke was arranged by his own countrymen,
and not by the terrorist Black Hand, the organization
of Serbian ultra-nationalists; that Gavrilo Princip, the
student terrorist who fired the fatal shots, was a tool of
the archduke's enemies at home.

Speculation always follows a major political murder;

and this speculation does not tend to die with time. In the United States, even after the official investigation into and report on the assassination of John F. Kennedy, there are still many who doubt the official version. Many also refuse to believe that the assassination of Martin Luther King, Jr., was plotted and carried out by a single individual. The speculation as to the responsibility for the murder of Franz Ferdinand in Sarajevo, however, was quickly, if temporarily, drowned out by the noises of marching feet, rolling guns, invasion, attack and counterattack, an all-consuming war on land, and war at sea.

It was a war in which millions would be killed, millions more maimed, and still more left homeless. Thrones would be toppled, empires destroyed, the face of Europe—physically and politically—torn up by revolution.

It was a war that had been a long time coming. Europe, in the forty years before Sarajevo, was rife with political intrigue, secret military pacts, clashing imperialist ambition. The Black Hand, with its secret terrorist program and action, and Gavrilo Princip, with his deadly aim in Sarajevo on June 28, 1914, paved the way, offering a logic, however faulty, for the mighty nations of Europe to give vent to their military antagonisms, to embark on the bloodiest holocaust that the continent—and the world—had yet experienced.

The Black Hand at Sarajevo is the story of that intrigue, the double-dealing, the struggle for power among the European nations which preceded the First World War. It is also the story of the Black Hand, its organization, its purpose, the manner in which it recruited and trained its assassins; the story of those assassins, almost all of them of schoolboy age, and how they perpetrated the most dramatic political murders in history.

THE BLACK HAND
AT SARAJEVO

Appointment in Sarajevo

ARCHDUKE Franz Ferdinand, heir to the throne of the Austro-Hungarian Empire, dictated a telegram to be delivered to his three children: "Papa and Mamma are well and look forward to being with you again next Thursday." It was the last note the three children—aged fourteen, eleven, and ten—would receive from their father. The telegram was dictated at Ilidze, a resort town just six miles from Sarajevo, in Bosnia; the date was June 28, 1914.

Bosnia, along with Hercegovina, was a province Austria-Hungary had annexed from Turkey in 1908. While the Moslems who inhabited the territory, about thirty percent of the population, were indifferent to the annexation, the Croat and Serbian Slavs, who constituted seventy percent of its inhabitants, were violently opposed to living under the Austrian flag. Openly and secretly they agitated for liberation from Austrian rule and for unification with the neighboring Slav country, Serbia. The secret agitation, from the very beginning, was violent and often terrorist in its character.

In 1910 a Serbian fired five shots at the Austrian governor of Bosnia, missed his target, and killed himself with the sixth bullet from his gun; he became a national hero for the Slav patriots. In 1912 the Slav terrorists were more successful; they assassinated the Croat secretary of education and, the next year, wounded the Austrian governor of Croatia.

General Oskar Potiorek, the Austrian governor of Bosnia in 1913, had countered the terrorist action with intensified police activity, with censorship of the press, and with temporary suspension of the territory's parliament. But such measures are not inclined to quiet a volatile situation; on the contrary, they serve to increase the tension and the unrest, and to create an atmosphere which frequently makes for greater violence.

In the summer of 1913 the general, for reasons which have never been entirely above suspicion, invited the Archduke Franz Ferdinand and his wife Sophie, Duchess of Hohenberg, to the province. He suggested in his invitation that the archduke, as inspector general of the Austrian army, supervise the scheduled maneuvers of the celebrated Fifteenth and Sixteenth Army Corps, the men who had guarded the Austrian borders so admirably during the Balkan Wars of 1912 and 1913; then, as heir to the throne of the empire, with his duchess, pay a one-day state visit to the provincial capital, Sarajevo.

In Vienna, capital of the Austro-Hungarian Empire, it was not difficult to read Potiorek's invitation as a request for help. A show of support by the royal family might well shore up the governor's campaign to put a leash on the irritating and dangerous activities of the nationalist Slav zealots. Certainly, a visit by the Archduke Franz Ferdinand would serve this purpose for the harassed general.

But, as Potiorek and everyone else knew, Bosnia, and particularly Sarajevo, was not the safest spot on the map for Austrian dignitaries, especially for members of the royal House of Hapsburg. Potiorek must have known, too, that the date for the proposed visit, late in June, was perhaps the worst of any for a demonstration of Austrian domination on what was considered by so many to be Slav soil. It was on St. Vitus's Day, June 28, 1389, that the Turks had utterly destroyed a Serbian army in the Battle of Kosovo, on the plains of southern Serbia, and put an end to Serbian independence for a period of almost five hundred years. It was a day whose significance no Serbian nationalist could forget. It was a day when Serbian nationalism, if provoked, could easily rise to fever pitch. It was a day, as Potiorek and others must have known, when violence in Sarajevo was not only possible but, realistically, most likely to occur. What made Potiorek's invitation even more suspect was the fact that the archduke had only comparatively recently blocked promotions for the general; once when he had been recommended for the post of chief of staff for the Austrian army, and again when he had been proposed for Austria's minister of war.

There are other elements in the story which raise suspicions concerning the general's motives in inviting the archduke to visit Sarajevo. Certainly the general's tactics, relating to that fateful day in June, the twenty-eighth, raise a number of possibly unanswerable questions. For one, there was a marked laxity of security in the streets of Sarajevo for the entourage of the visiting archduke. There had been a minimum of security arrests among the dangerous elements of the city prior to the archduke's arrival. There were definitely not enough police to monitor the huge crowds that turned out to welcome and cheer (and perhaps murder) the heir to the Austro-Hungarian throne. Most strangely, there was the specific order, issued by General Potiorek himself, which kept all but a handful of soldiers out of the Bosnian capital at the time of the archduke's presence. These are surely the kinds of facts which call for serious investigation after an assassination, but no such investigation followed the murders in Sarajevo. The world holocaust followed too quickly on the heels of the dramatic events of June 28, 1914.

The archduke did not respond immediately to Potiorek's invitation. He knew the Bosnian situation well enough. He knew Potiorek, too—well enough to consider the motives behind the invitation and to distrust them. However, it was neither Potiorek nor his possible designs which influenced Franz Ferdinand's response to the general. The archduke was a military man; he enjoyed his post as inspector general of the army and sometimes went out of his way to participate in army maneuvers. Nor did the terrorist activities in Bosnia initially deter his decision; the archduke was, if nothing else, a man of great courage. What enticed him most, and Potiorek was certainly clever enough to know it, was the prospect of a state visit, with his Duchess Sophie at his side. Sophie was not of royal blood and had been forced to suffer indignity after indignity at the court in Vienna; the archduke could not pass up this opportunity for the regal pomp and circumstance his wife could enjoy; the love of the archduke for his duchess, Sophie, was profound. He informed General Potiorek that he would be in Bosnia to supervise the army maneuvers, that the duchess and he would make the state visit to Sarajevo, as the general had asked.

Potiorek, of course, was delighted. Others, Serbians and his own countrymen, were disturbed by the announced visit of the archduke to Bosnia. Franz Ferdinand was an advocate of Trialism—the creation of a unified state of southern Slavs, with its capital at Zagreb, as an integral part of an Austro-Hungarian-Slav

Empire. This ran counter to the Serbian dream of a Greater Serbia that would include every community of Slavs, large or small, in the Balkans. Belgrade, the capital of Serbia, viewed the archduke's projected trip to Sarajevo as a threat to the profoundest of its ambitions; and Hungary, whose territory bordered on Serbia and who wanted no part of the Slavs in the empire, did not look kindly on the archduke's plans, either.

Still others, secretly and sometimes openly, looked forward to the presence of Franz Ferdinand in Sarajevo as an opportunity to strike a blow for Bosnia and independence. As early as December 3, 1913, a Serbian language paper, printed in Chicago, called on all Serbians to take advantage of the situation the archduke was about to offer them, to "seize everything you can lay your hands on—knives, rifles, bombs and dynamite! Take holy vengeance! Death to the Hapsburg dynasty!"

The archduke began to have second thoughts about the journey into the Balkans. He did not need the counsel of his few friends to know that he had enemies, both at home and abroad, men who feared the day he would assume the throne, men who would like to see him out of the way. Franz Ferdinand was never a man for the diplomatic gesture. Arrogant and impatient, he tended to care little for tact or soft speech, and his violent outbursts of temper did little to alleviate antagonisms.

"I assume," he said, "that everyone I meet is a scoundrel, until he proves to me that he is not."

There were few who could maintain a friendship with the strong-willed, aggressive, often morose Hapsburg, and with the death of his cousin Archduke Rudolf, the only son of the emperor and first heir to the throne, Franz Ferdinand turned more belligerent, more morose, more distrustful. Rudolf, a Prince Charming, a sensitive, brooding intellectual, had been particularly friendly toward his withdrawn younger cousin, solicitous of his welfare. On January 30, 1889, at his hunting lodge in Mayerling, for reasons which have never been clarified because of official censorship, Rudolf killed his young mistress Maria Vetsena, then killed himself.

Through the years violent death had plagued the House of Hapsburg. Maximilian, the emperor's brother, who himself had been crowned Emperor of Mexico in 1864, was taken prisoner in the Mexican revolution which followed shortly after, tried and convicted by a Mexican revolutionary court, and executed in 1867. The emperor's beautiful wife, Elizabeth, was assassinated in Geneva, Switzerland, by the crazed twenty-six-year-old anarchist Luigi Lucheni on September 10, 1898. Franz Ferdinand had no recollection of his uncle's execution; the assassination of his aunt had a marked effect on his relationship with his wife Sophie; but it was the suicide of his cousin which abruptly changed the course of his life.

With the death of Rudolf, Franz Ferdinand became the heir to the throne of the Austro-Hungarian Empire, although his status did not become official until the death of his father, Carl Ludwig, some seven years later. It was a responsibility for which he had very little taste and for which physically he was not too well equipped. When he was a young man his state of health had never been good. He had a throat ailment which had never been completely remedied and which forced him to take frequent trips to milder and drier climates than Vienna's. At one time his personal physician diagnosed his illness as tuberculosis and told him that he did not have much longer to live; and to the archduke's considerable displeasure the court in Vienna began to look with scarcely concealed satisfaction to Otto, Franz Ferdinand's handsome, popular younger brother as heir to the throne. But Franz Ferdinand was possessed of a particularly strong and stubborn will; he would not die of tuberculosis, nor would he allow his chronic ailments to interfere with his customary vigorous athletic activity.

His will and his inordinate stubbornness, however, did not sit well with the aging Emperor Franz Josef. The emperor had never looked kindly on his nephew. In fact he avoided him, making him feel, in some unreasonable manner, that he was responsible for the death of his cousin Rudolf. The emperor's coolness, even cruelty, was most marked, however, in the attitude he took to the one great romance in the life of the heir to his throne.

Franz Ferdinand was not the romantic that his cousin Rudolf was; nor was he given to the kind of philandering common to the court in Vienna. He fell in love with Sophie von Chotkova und Wognin, a mere lady in waiting, and despite much opposition—from the emperor down to the court of Vienna—he married her on July 1, 1900. It was a morganatic marriage, the marriage between a member of the royal house and a commoner, and the archduke was required to take an oath which declared, in part, that neither his wife nor any of their descendants possessed the "right to succeed to the Throne" of the empire. And the only members of the royal family to attend the wedding were Franz Ferdinand's stepmother Maria Theresa and her two daughters. There were other humiliations which Franz Ferdinand and, especially, his wife were to endure in their otherwise most happy marriage.

Sophie, a tall, handsome, proud beauty with dark hair

and dark eyes, found herself seated at the lower end of the table at court dinners. She was always at the tail end of the processions at the court balls. She was not even allowed to ride with her husband in the royal carriage. The indignities that his wife had to suffer became a little too much for the archduke to take, and as the gap of understanding between Franz Ferdinand and the emperor widened, he began to avoid both Vienna and the court whenever possible.

The opportunity to ride in state with his wife, to be greeted royally with his wife at his side, to enjoy the ceremonials of a state visit together, undoubtedly had been a pleasing prospect for the proud archduke in his first thoughts on the prospective trip to Bosnia. It was Pope Pius X who had said of Franz Ferdinand, "He sees through the eyes of his wife." But as the date for the journey drew nearer and it was suggested that he leave Sophie at home, considering the uncertainties of the situation in the Austrian province, his enthusiasm for the trek lessened considerably. He would go with Sophie or not at all. And for a while it seemed that it might very well be not at all.

Early in the spring of 1914, he had taken Sophie and their three children on a motor car tour through a region of Austria close to the borders of Italy. It was a territory claimed by Italian Irredentists, nationalists as zealous and as violent as the Slav nationalists in Bosnia. Colonel Carl von Bardolff, one of his military aides, had cautioned him on the dangers involved in such an excursion, but Franz Ferdinand had been almost strangely stoical in his response.

"I'm sure you're right, but we can't live our lives in constant fear. We can only trust in God."

But the persistent friendly words of caution and the endless number of rumors in and around the court predicting violence in Sarajevo—however little credence he gave them—began to mark his thinking. His aunt, his uncle, and his cousin had died violently; if he had no fear for his own life, there was Sophie to consider, and the three children to whom he was deeply devoted.

He received repeated reports from General Oskar Potiorek that all was well in Bosnia, that peace and order prevailed. But Franz Ferdinand was not impressed. He had little respect for the general and trusted him less. He became more morose, more irritable. When he received word from Colonel Bardolff of a minor change in his Bosnian schedule, he tore up his handkerchief in a rage and shouted, "Tell the Colonel that if there are any more changes, he can hold the maneuvers himself! I won't go at all!"

On June 4, 1914, with his journey to Sarajevo due to start in about three weeks, he sought an audience with the Emperor Franz Josef to speak of his doubts.

The summer heat in Bosnia would be unbearable. The rugged terrain in which the army maneuvers were to be held, with no trees and no water, might have an ill effect on his throat. Perhaps, for reasons of health, he had better cancel the project. He did not once mention, of course, what was uppermost in his mind: his forebodings concerning the very real possibility of an assassination plot; but such fears would hardly be becoming to a Hapsburg, especially the heir to the throne of Austria-Hungary.

What the old and ailing emperor was thinking, and how much of the archduke's dissertation he heard, is difficult to estimate. His reply, to the obvious discomfort of his nephew, was noncommittal.

"Do as you please."

The choice was the archduke's; or so it seemed. But

Franz Ferdinand had asked the emperor to release him from what had become an assignment in Bosnia; and the emperor had turned down his request. The archduke and his wife Sophie would keep their appointment in Sarajevo.

Assassination

FRANZ FERDINAND was a devout Catholic. He believed that the throne of Austria-Hungary, with all its burdens, would be his by God's will. He believed that in all things, large or small, God's will would be done. Despite all the forebodings of tragedy that would not leave him, on the day of his departure for Bosnia it was undoubtedly his faith in the Lord which had him in good spirits, even cheerful. Whatever else he might think, whatever and whomever he might question, there was never any wavering of his belief, his faith, and his trust in his God.

However, in what certainly appears to have been a presentiment of the fate waiting for him in Sarajevo, he indulged himself in what was for the archduke an unusual gesture. He called Franz Janaczek, his trusted and faithful valet, into his chambers and presented him with a solid gold watch.

"Should anything happen to me," he said, "I would wish you to stay with the duchess, and with our children."

Janaczek would be faithful to his trust. He had taken his last orders and his last request from his master the archduke.

Taking the usual fond farewells from their children,

who were accustomed to the frequent comings and goings of their much-traveled parents, the archduke and his wife left their castle in Chlumetz to board the Vienna express for the capital. But here they ran into the first of a series of odd accidents which were to mark their journey.

A few miles out of Chlumetz, the archduke's private parlor car had been coupled to the express, a procedure that could have been repeated any number of times without incident. This day, however, June 23, 1914, one of the parlor car's journal boxes had inexplicably become overheated. Smoke billowed from it, and the porter in charge at the station, a faithful and conscientious man, was frantic with frustration. He made profuse apologies to the archduke, repeatedly and humbly, but all he could do in the situation was to remove the royal parlor car and offer the archduke and the duchess seats in the first-class compartment of the train.

"This is a promising beginning," said the archduke, rather cynically, and he must have wondered whether worse lay ahead for him and his wife Sophie.

Arriving in Vienna without any further mishap on that express train, they drove to the Belvedere Castle, their Vienna residence; and from there, according to the protocol of their day, their itineraries separated. Franz Ferdinand was to go by train to Trieste; by battleship from Trieste across the Adriatic to the River Narenta, then on to the small town of Metkovic; finally, by train again to Ilidze in Bosnia.

The duchess went directly by train to Ilidze, and except for the crowds of people who gathered at the stop-stations to catch a glimpse of the lady, her trip was uneventful. Not so the archduke's journey.

At Südbahnhof, the station from which Franz Ferdinand was to entrain for Trieste, the station master had replaced the archduke's private car with another, as requested. But, as outside of Chlumetz, Franz Ferdinand was again confronted by a nervous, apologetic railroad official. It was the electric wiring this time—again without any explainable cause—which had failed. And it was impossible even to try to make the necessary repairs, if the train was to leave on schedule.

"Would the archduke object very much to the use of candles to illuminate the car?"

"What do you think of this lighting?" the archduke asked the secretary who had accompanied him to the station. "It looks like a grave, doesn't it?"

There can be no question that Franz Ferdinand interpreted the accidents at Chlumetz and Südbahnhof as portents of something infinitely worse; still, his thoughts were with his duchess, and his final words to his secretary were, "Look after Her Highness. See to it that she gets to Ilidze safely."

On June 24, at Trieste, the archduke boarded the battleship *Viribus Unitis,* sailed across a calm Adriatic and, after an eighteen-hour trip, transferred to the smaller warship *Dalmat,* where General Oskar Potiorek was waiting to greet him. The *Dalmat*'s course was up the River Narenta, and on both sides of the stream were crowds of people, flags and bunting, the waving of hands, cheering, and the firing of salutes from every town they passed. Things began to look a little brighter for the archduke as the ship approached the little town of Metkovic, where Franz Ferdinand was to take a special train to Ilidze and the waiting Sophie.

There was a short stop, however, in Metkovic for a quick official reception. There was a longer stopover at Mostar, the next station on the line. The long-winded mayor of the city had to make a welcoming address:

"I most humbly thank Your Royal Highness for the gracious visit being paid to our city and I pray that God may grant health and a long happy life to Your Royal and Imperial Highness . . ."

There was a band at the station, too, and all the town's dignitaries.

Franz Ferdinand may have enjoyed the various expressions of loyalty and good will, or he may have been eager to be done with them and on his way to his wife. But protocol demanded his forbearance, and it was two hours before he could leave Mostar, the capital of Hercegovina and a remarkably beautiful city with its sixteen thousand mosques and pristine, whitewashed houses.

Despite a steady rainfall, there was another huge crowd, another band, another reception at Ilidze, where the train arrived on schedule at three in the afternoon. Feeling considerably better now—the forebodings of evil forgotten for the moment—Franz Ferdinand had a kind word for each of the military and civil dignitaries who had come to welcome him, as he reviewed the guard of honor assembled at the station. He was actually exuberant, meeting again with Sophie in the hotel suite which had been elaborately prepared for the royal visitors. The hostility he might well have anticipated was nowhere in evidence; instead, there were salutes and cheers and extremely gratifying expressions of good will and loyalty. It seemed that his concerns and his misgivings had been idle and completely unnecessary apprehensions. He intended to make his visit to Bosnia a happy holiday for himself and for Sophie, and he meant to begin at once.

Only hours after his arrival in Ilidze, the archduke and his wife traveled the six miles to Sarajevo on a shopping trip. If he took the time to read the Sarajevo newspapers, he knew that his little journey into town had brought out a cheering populace.

"Be Greeted, Illustrious Prince!" ran the headline in the Sarajevo Moslem journals.

"Hail to You!" was the banner line in the Croat newspaper.

"Hail to the Heir Apparent!" was the contribution of the Serb publications.

Zivio!—the Serb-Croat equivalent of *Hurrah!*—was the welcome shout of the people who appeared in droves to mark the impromptu visit of Franz Ferdinand and his wife as they moved with some difficulty through the milling throng in and around Sarajevo's famous Oriental Bazaar.

It was at the Bazaar that the archduke, aware only of the warmth and happiness that surrounded him, unknowingly came face to face with an intensely zealous Slav nationalist, the young Black Hand assassin-to-be who was to leave his name well marked in history. But on that afternoon, June 25, 1914, there was nothing, except perhaps for the excessive pushing and shoving of an enthusiastic people, to mar the increasingly joyous mood of the archduke.

There had been no opportunity for the authorities to assign a special security guard for the royal couple on their quick excursion into Sarajevo; they had had no warning of the archduke's impulsive gesture; and this was much to Franz Ferdinand's liking. He preferred to move about freely among the people, without security police at his heels. In fact, he avoided security guards and escaped them whenever he could.

Twenty special policeman were assigned to ensure his safety during the army maneuvers of the Fifteenth and Sixteenth Corps, which took place on the twenty-sixth and the twenty-seventh some ten miles west of

Ilidze. It rained, hailed, and snowed in the barren and mountainous region of Bosnia without letup those two days, and with the archduke's riding off abruptly first in one direction, then in another, the special guard had difficulty keeping him in sight. After a while, the security police gave up on their mission and became as lax as the archduke about safety precautions.

At one point in the maneuvers, a civilian suddenly appeared, seemingly out of nowhere, and began to run toward the archduke's car. There was no one near, policeman or soldier, to stop him, and it was Franz Ferdinand himself who first spotted the intruder.

Apparently without fear, he ordered his chauffeur to halt his car and wait for the stranger to approach.

He might have been a nationalist, a terrorist, an assassin; he was only a peddler, however, who claimed to be a follower of army maneuvers. Relieved, even amused, the archduke bought some picture cards and some trinkets from him and sent him on his way.

A police officer was close by, though, when at another time during the maneuvers a man with a long black tube in his hands jumped out of the shrubbery in the hills. The officer was quick enough to grab the man by his collar. Franz Ferdinand took one quick look at the unfortunate intruder and began to laugh.

"Let him go," he ordered the tense security guard. "He's the court photographer. Let him go!"

Actually, the twenty-two-thousand-man maneuvers went very well, probably better than the archduke had expected. And Franz Ferdinand, though he at all times preferred peace to war, enjoyed army games. He sent a special message of congratulations on their performances to the men of the corps, with special thanks to General Potiorek and all the other officers. He sent a rather glowing report on the corps, too, to the Emperor

Franz Josef. Then he returned to Sophie, who had been enjoying her stay, visiting the churches, the schools, and the orphanages of Sarajevo, being cordially received wherever she went.

The evening of the twenty-seventh of June, their last scheduled evening in Bosnia, was given to a formal dinner party. Dr. Josip Sunaric, vice-president of Bosnia's parliament, attended that dinner. He had been one of those who had counseled the Hapsburgs to avoid the province because of the potentially dangerous mood of the Slavs. Sophie made a point of speaking to him at the dinner.

"Dear Dr. Sunaric," she said, smiling at him broadly, "you were wrong after all. Things don't always turn out the way you might imagine. We have been greeted everywhere with such friendliness—even by Serbs—and with so much cordiality and warmth; and we are very happy for it."

The astute doctor replied politely but earnestly, "Your Highness, I pray to God that when I have the honor of seeing you again tomorrow night, you can repeat those words to me. I shall breathe easier then, a great deal easier."

The good doctor knew what he was talking about. The stay of the Hapsburgs in Bosnia was not yet at an end. There was still the state visit to Sarajevo which Sophie and her archduke husband were to make the following morning.

As the guests began to leave the dinner party toward midnight, Franz Ferdinand, still thoroughly pleased both with the reception Sophie and he had received in the province and with his participation in the army maneuvers, remarked rather casually, though perhaps a little wearily, "It has all been very pleasant, but I shall be glad to get back to Chlumetz."

One of his aides seized on the remark to suggest that he forget Sarajevo and leave in the morning; and the archduke, who often enough made abrupt changes in his travel itineraries, thought it might not be a bad idea at all to take the train out of Ilidze and proceed directly to Vienna, then home.

But others in the entourage objected. The people of Sarajevo had been keyed up for the prospective state visit by the archduke and his duchess. They would feel keenly disappointed, deeply slighted, if the visit were cancelled. And General Potiorek, who was responsible for all the elaborate preparations for the royal visit, might very well be offended if the archduke left Bosnia without the planned reception in its capital city.

It may have been the hour; it may have been his weariness after the long days with the Fifteenth and Sixteenth Corps; most likely it was indifference. "Let's keep to the schedule as it is," he said, and retired for the night.

The schedule prepared for the archduke and his wife called for an early-morning departure from Ilidze; a brief review of the troops stationed in the Philipovic army camp on the outskirts of Sarajevo; a motor car ride through the streets of the town to its town hall for a brief reception; an hour at Sarajevo's National Museum; at 12:30 P.M., a farewell lunch at the residence of the governor; then back to Ilidze, from which, at 9:00 P.M., they would entrain for Vienna. It was a full schedule and tightly timed.

A private room at their hotel was set up for Sunday mass, at which Franz Ferdinand and Sophie were in attendance. Repairing to his private chambers, the archduke dictated the last telegrams he would ever send, including the message he sent to his children, who had remained in Chlumetz. Then the archduke, his wife, and their retinue, walked to the railroad station and, at 9:25 A.M., left on their special train for Sarajevo.

In Sarajevo, a proclamation by the mayor was posted on more than a hundred walls. It began:

"Citizens!

"His Imperial and Royal Highness, our Most Gracious Successor Archduke Franz Ferdinand, will honor our city with his illustrious visit. Our deep-rooted feelings of filial gratitude, devotion, fidelity and loyalty to His Imperial and Royal Apostolic Majesty . . ."

The proclamation also posted the streets "through which His Highness will pass," and it was along these streets that the Sarajevo police worked frantically, not fixing security measures, but tearing down anti-Hapsburg signs, anti-Austrian banners, and the Serbian flags that had suddenly blossomed all over the city and particularly along the announced route of the archduke and his entourage. As for the actual security arrangements for the royal visit, there were scarcely more than token preparations, certainly not enough to handle the kind of mass reception that must have been expected to greet Austria's heir to the throne.

When Emperor Franz Josef had visited Sarajevo in 1910, there had been more than two hundred preventive arrests of malcontents who might prove dangerous to the emperor's person. A good number of others, citizens of Sarajevo, had been ordered to remain indoors for the duration of his visit. The entire garrison of troops stationed in Sarajevo had been detailed to line its streets as the emperor passed through, making it impossible for any large crowds to gather on the narrow pavements.

It was quite different on the morning of June 28, 1914. There had been only thirty-five preventive arrests. No one was ordered to remain indoors. The streets of Sarajevo had been declared off-limits for the army garrison so long as the archduke was in town, and the entire security force assigned for the occasion was limited to no more than one hundred twenty uniformed policemen and plainclothes detectives.

The Emperor Franz Josef had not been pleased with the strictness of the security prepared for his visit, and at times he disregarded it, moving right through the guards and into the crowds. And Franz Ferdinand, as General Potiorek knew, didn't like anything resembling a security guard. Perhaps his experience with the emperor and his knowledge of the archduke's likes and dislikes were factors in the general's security preparations, but there was no excuse for the completely inadequate, utterly unrealistic security measures Potiorek arranged for that fateful morning.

The general was at the station when the train pulled into Sarajevo from Ilidze. He escorted the archduke and his retinue the short distance from the railroad station to where Franz Ferdinand reviewed the corps under the command of Michael von Appel. Then, according to schedule, the archduke and his welcoming party got into their cars for the ride through the city to the town hall.

There were six cars in the procession. The mayor of Sarajevo, Effendi Curcic, and the commissioner of police, Dr. Edmund Gerde, were in the lead car. Next came the oversized grey touring car with the black and yellow flag of Austria flying in the wind. Franz Count Harrach, member of the Austro-Hungarian Voluntary Automobile Corps, sat next to its chauffeur. In the rear seats of the car sat the archduke and his wife, the archduke dressed in his military tunic and general's headdress, a tumble of green cock feathers in his helmet; the duchess in a broad-brimmed picture hat and high-necked white dress. The archduke did wear a specially constructed bulletproof vest, but his head and his neck were unprotected, and he made an easy target for any would-be assassin, especially with his car's top rolled down to allow the crowds a better view of the visiting royalty.

In the third car of the procession rode Countess Lanjus, lady in waiting to the duchess; Colonel von Bardolff; Lieutenant Colonel Erik von Merizzi, General Potiorek's chief aide; and Count Alexander von Boos-Waldeck.

The third and fourth cars carried various other dignitaries, Austrian and Bosnian; the fifth, an extra car in case of some emergency, was empty except for its chauffeur.

The entourage moved at a leisurely pace down Appel Quay, the widest street in Sarajevo, along the Miljacka River. A huge crush of people thronged the walks, eager to get a glimpse of the royalty. The summer sun warmed the streets, a welcome change after a week of rain and cold; the houses along the way were decorated lavishly and colorfully with flowers and flags, many with blown-up pictures of the archduke. All was proper, all was festive, the crowds cheering *Zivio!* as the procession approached and then passed by. Then, abruptly, as General Potiorek indicated to the archduke the new army barracks across the Cumurja Bridge, a bomb came hurtling out of the crowd, directly at the car carrying the royal passengers.

Franz Ferdinand instinctively raised his hand to protect his wife. His arm deflected the murderous missile, and the bomb fell on the folded roof of his car, bounced into the street, and exploded, filling the air with smoke and shrapnel. Franz Ferdinand, untouched by the assassin's bomb, ordered his car stopped. There was bedlam in the streets. Women fainted. Sophie's face had been scratched by a flying fragment, but she was too distraught to notice it. It was the car directly behind the archduke's which took the brunt of the punishment. Countess Lanjus had been struck by one of the bomb's splinters, and Count von Boos-Waldeck had taken a number of fragments; neither was seriously wounded. Lieutenant Colonel Merizzi, however, had been hit in the back of the head and was bleeding profusely.

Dr. Fischer, the archduke's physician, who had been riding in the fourth car, examined the wound quickly and ordered that the lieutenant colonel be taken immediately to a nearby physician. Before he could be removed, however, Major Arnstein, the doctor in charge of the Sarajevo army garrison, arrived with three army surgeons to attend the dozen onlookers who had been hit by bomb fragments. They took a quick look at Colonel Merizzi and ordered an ambulance to take him to the army hospital.

The entourage then quickened its pace, leaving the one crippled car behind, and proceeded at once—without further incident—to the town hall. It had been intended that the formal reception be a joyous affair; the bombing, of course, had made everyone tense.

The archduke was not one to conceal his displeasure or his anger. "Mr. Mayor," he snapped, before the mayor could even begin his carefully prepared welcome speech, "we come to visit you and we are greeted with bombs! This is outrageous."

There was a seemingly endless pause, as the archduke tried to collect himself.

"All right," he said, breaking the unnerving silence, "you may speak now."

Either the mayor was too frightened to alter his

speech to meet the critical moment, or else he had not the intelligence to do so. In any case, he read his prepared text verbatim.

"Your Royal and Imperial Highness! Your Highness! Our hearts are full of happiness . . . and I consider myself happy that Your Highnesses can read in our faces the feelings of our love and devotion, our unshakable loyalty. . . . All the citizens of Sarajevo find their souls are filled with happiness and they most enthusiastically greet Your Highnesses' most illustrious visit with the most cordial of welcomes. . . . Welcome! Long live our beloved and most exalted guests: His Royal and Imperial Highness, the Most Serene Archduke Heir Apparent Franz Ferdinand, and Her Highness Duchess Sophie! . . ."

It was hardly to be expected that the archduke would be amused by the mayor's bumbling address, certainly an inappropriate one for the occasion. But he was gracious, if cynical, in his response:

"I thank you cordially for the resounding ovations with which the population received me and my wife, the more so since I see in them an expression of pleasure over the failure of the assassination attempt."

More kindly, he closed with, "May I ask you to give my cordial greetings to the inhabitants of this beautiful capital city, and may I assure you of my unchanged regard and favor."

The crowd that had gathered at the town hall cheered perhaps a little more enthusiastically than the formal occasion demanded, because of its tension; the archduke managed a smile, and the strain relaxed a bit.

Franz Ferdinand inquired after the condition of Lieutenant Colonel Merizzi and was pleased to hear that his wounds were superficial. He asked whether the man who had thrown the bomb had been apprehended. When told that he had been, the archduke remarked rather wryly, "Instead of putting him away, they will probably, in true Austrian fashion, award him the medal of merit."

It was suggested by some members of his entourage that the scheduled trip to the National Museum be dropped, for it would be too dangerous to drive through the narrow and crowded Sarajevo streets again. General Potiorek and the police commissioner didn't think another attack was likely, but still Potiorek thought the archduke might forget the museum trip and drive directly through the wider Appel Quay to Konak, the governor's residence, for the scheduled farewell lunch.

Franz Ferdinand saw no reason to change the plans, but first he did want to visit Merizzi at the hospital.

One of the archduke's aides suggested a wait in the town hall until the streets could be emptied and at least two companies of soldiers from the garrison could be stationed in the city.

Potiorek vetoed the suggestion. The police at hand were not adequate to clear the streets, and the troops were not in the dress which the presence of the archduke required.

Franz Ferdinand did attempt one precautionary measure—not for himself, but for his wife. He asked Baron von Morsey to take Sophie either straight to the governor's residence or directly back to Ilidze. But Sophie would hear of neither; she would stay with the archduke as long as they remained in Sarajevo.

The procession left the town hall in the same order as it had arrived, with the mayor's car in the lead, the archduke's car following. This time, however, Count Harrach of the Voluntary Automobile Corps rode on the left running board of the archduke's car, serving as a shield for the royalty, since it was from the left that the bomb had been thrown.

Again the crowd cheered *Zivio!* as the cars moved past. At Franz Josef Street, the mayor's chauffeur made a right turn. Evidently he had not been told that the orders had been changed, that he was to drive straight down Appel Quay to the hospital. The chauffeur of the archduke's car followed.

"The wrong way!" shouted General Potiorek. "Where are you going? We're to go down Appel Quay!"

The chauffeur stepped on his brakes, then backed his car slowly for the turn. The maneuver put the car, moving at its slow pace, directly in line with a waiting young Bosnian Slav zealot—the one the archduke had encountered at the Oriental Bazaar on his unscheduled first visit to Sarajevo—Gavrilo Princip. Princip was no more than five feet away from an almost stationary target.

Princip stepped forward, pulled his gun, and fired twice. The first bullet struck the Duchess of Hohenberg in the abdomen. The second hit the archduke's neck and pierced his jugular vein.

Count Harrach had been standing on the wrong side of the car.

For a moment, the archduke and the duchess continued to sit upright, as if it were undignified to react to the assassin's bullets. But when blood began to flow from the wounded archduke's mouth, Sophie cried out, "What has happened to you?" Then she sank down from her seat, her head coming to rest at the archduke's knees.

Franz Ferdinand, who knew very well what had happened to him, turned to his wife and earnestly pleaded with her to stay alive.

"*Sopherl! Sopherl!* Don't die! Stay alive for our children!"

Count Harrach tried to hold the archduke erect.

"Are you suffering much, Your Imperial Highness?"

"It's nothing," the archduke responded, but he was fast growing weak. "It's nothing."

Franz Ferdinand and Sophie were barely alive when they arrived at the governor's residence, to which they had been rushed. Sophie, however, was perhaps already dead of an internal hemorrhage when they carried her to the governor's bedroom. Franz Ferdinand, on a couch in an adjoining room, lingered on in a deep coma, barely breathing, for a little while. For a few moments after they had loosened his tight bulletproof vest, his breathing seemed to be a bit stronger, and there was a sudden ray of hope for his life. But within twenty minutes of the death of his wife, the archduke was dead. The flowers that had been prepared for the farewell lunch at the governor's residence came to rest on the still bodies of the two who were to have been the guests of honor.

While there had been political assassinations before —and there would be political assassinations after— none had ever proved so critical to the history of the world. Within a little more than a month Europe's most powerful nations were joined in a bloody holocaust that would soon involve almost all of the world.

It cannot be said that the assassination in Sarajevo on June 28, 1914, was the cause of the terrible bloodshed which followed; rather, it was more a match to the fuse of a bomb that had long been waiting to explode on the European continent. The force of that explosion would spread death in dreadful numbers among the guilty and the innocent alike.

The Prussian Position   3

HEADSTRONG, aggressive, arrogant, and intolerant, Kaiser Wilhelm II, Emperor of the Imperial German Empire, was generally regarded by his enemies as the villain, the instigator of what was initially called "the Great European War." In a considerable measure, he merited the accusations. But Britain, France, Russia, Italy, and the smaller nations of the turbulent continent were not entirely blameless in the terrible bloodshed that followed the assassination in Sarajevo.

The actual causes for the great war, which had been brewing in Europe for decades before Gavrilo Princip fired his gun at the archduke of Austria, were many and varied and far from subtle. There was the burgeoning, jingoistic nationalism which constantly threatened the long-established boundary lines of every major power on the Continent, as well as the rumblings of nationalist ambitions among the awakening smaller nations, particularly in the Balkans, the region which included Rumania, Bulgaria, Greece, and Serbia. There were rivalries among the big powers for colonial possessions in Africa and Asia, for spheres of influence, for raw materials and markets. There were the huge military build-ups, taking place at a steadily increasing pace, and a struggle for the control of the seas. And in France there was the unquenchable desire to reclaim from Germany Alsace-Lorraine, the territory it had been forced to cede to Prussia following its defeat at the hands of the Prussians in the War of 1870–71. Still, Germany might very well have delayed, if not averted, the great bloodletting which began in the midsummer of 1914.

Until 1866 Germany was composed of a number of small and separate independent kingdoms and principalities, kept divided designedly by the big powers— France, Russia, and Britain—to ensure a central Europe too weak to constitute any kind of rivalry to their own ambitions on the Continent or elsewhere. The Congress of Vienna, in 1815, which had assembled after the defeat of Napoleon Bonaparte, reshaped the map of Europe, establishing a balance-of-power relationship which was to last for about one hundred years. It also established the Germanic Confederation of some thirty-eight German states, including the comparatively powerful Austria. It was a loose organization which was virtually without power, since it required unanimous agreement for any kind of joint action. Austria presided over the Confederation and for some fifty years was able to maintain its dominance among the German states, despite a growingly aggressive German Prussia.

In 1866, however, under the guidance of the astute and brilliant Prince Otto von Bismarck, the Prussians disrupted the status quo and the Germanic Confederation as well. Taking advantage of the domestic difficulties in both Britain and Russia (the two powers which might have thwarted his plans), Bismarck instigated a war between Austria and Prussia over the control of the territory of Schleswig-Holstein. Schleswig-Holstein was originally part of Denmark, but was under joint Austro-Prussian control at the time. Differences about this control rose between Prussia and Austria, differences which might easily have been settled amicably; but Bismarck was for a test of strength between the two countries, and the war was the result.

Without the forces of the British or the Russians to keep the central European peace, the Prussians had little difficulty defeating the Austrians in a matter of only seven weeks. Kaiser Wilhelm I of Prussia desired the utter defeat of the Austrian nation, but Bismarck, wisely knowing such action would certainly cause the British and the Russians to intercede, persuaded his king to content himself with the quick victory.

It was a victory of no mean proportions. The Germanic Confederation, in which Austria dominated, was no more. In its place Bismarck created a North German Confederation, which excluded Austria and established the leadership of Prussia in central Europe, a power with which to be reckoned.

In 1870 Bismarck precipitated a second war, this time against the France of Napoleon III. Again the calculating statesman laid his plans well. Napoleon III, with dreams of glory inspired by his uncle, Napoleon I, had indicated his desire to take over Belgium and Luxembourg, a design which considerably disturbed Britain. Britain was always concerned with a possible imbalance of power in Europe. Russia, which had despised the French republic, eyed with suspicion any potential development of France's strength on the Continent. In addition, the Russians were still smarting over the aid the French had given the Poles in their unsuccessful revolution against Russia in 1863. Bismarck was certain that, at the very least, he could expect a benevolent neutrality on the part of Britain and Russia in the event of a Franco-Prussian war. He did better than that. Not only did the Russians promise to urge support for the

Prussians from the southern German states of Baden, Bavaria, Württemberg, and Hesse, but they pledged three hundred thousand troops along their Austrian border to ensure Austrian neutrality.

Bismarck knew that he didn't have enough military strength to fight on two fronts, but—with his rear secured by Russian promises—he provoked Napoleon III into a declaration of war. It proved a disastrous war for France.

With his rear secure, Helmuth von Moltke (Bismarck's general) was able to send an extra one hundred thousand men against the French; at Sedan he not only administered a crushing defeat to the French army, but also captured its emperor, Napoleon III. The fighting continued into 1871, but for all purposes Bismarck and the Prussians were once more victorious. France had to pay for its defeat by ceding the coal- and iron-rich Alsace to the Prussians, as well as Lorraine, with its city of Metz—the strongest fortress in Europe. To cap all his triumphs, Bismarck was to see Kaiser Wilhelm of Prussia crowned Kaiser Wilhelm I of a united Germany, with himself as its first chancellor. The Northern German Confederation had given way to a German empire which included the southern as well as the northern Germanic states.

With Germany now the principal power in central Europe—economically, politically, and militarily—Bismarck was content to consolidate his position. He called together the Congress of Europe to put a leash on Russian strength in the east, following Russia's defeat of Turkey in 1878. It was this Congress which gave Rumania and Serbia complete independence from the Ottoman Empire (Turkey), gave Cyprus to Britain, and placed Bosnia and Hercegovina under Austrian military and economic control. In 1879, the next year, he made a secret alliance with Austria which required Austria to support Germany in the event of an attack by France; Germany, in turn, was to support Austria if the Russians attacked her soil. Italy joined this dual alliance three years later, despite that nation's traditional antagonism toward Austria. It did so most likely for reasons of prestige, and certainly to gain support for its rivalry with the French for territory in Africa. Bismarck also renewed what was called the Three Emperors' League, a loose pledge of friendship among the Russians, the Austrians, and the Germans, which would not seem to hold in the face of the different secret pacts which had been formulated and signed.

Secret diplomacy, bordering on conspiracy, was the order of the day and certainly did not make for tranquility or stability in Europe. As for the Balkans, which were the focus of considerable European rivalry and turmoil—and which eventually was to prove at least the pretext for the testing of all the secret diplomacy and alliances—Bismarck was for a hands-off policy. The Balkans, he said, were not worth "the bones of a single Pomeranian grenadier." He would have liked Russia and Austria to divide the whole tumultuous area between them. Under no circumstance, he insisted, should Germany ever get involved in a war because of the Balkan question.

All of that changed with the death of Wilhelm I of Germany, and the crowning of Wilhelm II, following the death of his father Frederick III, who ruled in Germany for only three months until his death of cancer in 1888. If anything, Wilhelm II was more arrogant, more headstrong, more aggressive than Bismarck. He may well have appreciated the past works of the statesman, but he would play figurehead to no one. The break between the two stubborn men came quickly. In 1890

Wilhelm II dismissed Bismarck. German foreign policy, following 1890, would be in the hands of the emperor. It was a jingoist policy, filled with dreams and talk of German racial superiority and German destiny, its ultimate goal being the unification of all German people— in Switzerland, Austria, and even America—into one "greater Germany." There were other "greater" movements in Europe at the time. The Russian Nicholas Danilevsky had promulgated the idea of Pan-Slavism, the unification of all Slavs under Russian rule, in 1871. The "Greater Serbia" movement was to come later. Each helped create the great European conflagration of 1914.

Nor was Britain without fault in this dangerous race for national dominance, though by the time of Wilhelm II its possessions already ranged across the face of the earth, and the phrase "the sun never sets on the Union Jack" represented the truth. It was with a Britain which was perfectly satisfied to keep a balance and a peace in the world that Kaiser Wilhelm II had his most immediate differences, and in a number of different areas.

With a tremendously developing industrial capacity, he challenged British markets around the world, as far away as Latin America and China. Bismarck had procured Germany's first colonies in Africa; Wilhelm was for expanding those holdings to challenge British and French domination on that continent. During the Boer War, involving the British and the original Dutch settlers, the kaiser went so far as to disparage the British and encourage the Boers. And despite Bismarck's caution, he entered the Balkan muddle by declaring himself the friend of the three hundred million Moslems who inhabited the earth.

He went further, antagonizing both the Russians and the British by an open declaration of *Drang Nach Osten*

—"push to the east"—and his intention to build a railroad from Berlin to Bagdad. A German military mission was sent to Turkey to reorganize and reconstruct its army, thereby putting the Turkish armed forces virtually under German command.

The kaiser was not only challenging British as well as French and Russian commerce, he was taking over their spheres of influence and military domination. In Morocco he almost clashed with Spain, as well as with France, and a naval battle between Germany on the one side and the United States and Britain on the other was averted only by a sudden and destructive storm in the seas of the South Pacific Samoan Islands. Wilhelm II was rattling his swords, apparently without fear.

The kaiser had already developed the largest standing army in the world. Next came his challenge to Britain as Mistress of the Seas. In 1897 the Germans announced a five-year shipbuilding program whose purpose, according to their secretary of the Navy, Admiral Alfred von Tirpitz, was not equality but the creation of a navy strong enough to threaten serious damage to the most powerful navies in the world, one that no other navy would dare attack. The kaiser declared that the trident (symbol of Neptune, god of the seas) would be in his hand. There could be no doubt in Britain that the words of the admiral and of the kaiser were directed at the British; and Britain had to be concerned. Its sea forces would have to be completely revamped, after so many years of inactivity, to meet the Germans' boastful challenge. And the kaiser had widened the sixty-mile Kiel Canal, the artificial waterway which connected the Baltic Sea with the North Sea, and which by 1895 was broad enough to allow German battleships to move from their dockings into open sea battle with any potential antagonist.

Bismarck had fashioned a strong and united Germany and had made her a power in the European world. He had made an enemy of France, but he had also managed, in his intricate agreements with Russia, Austria, and Italy, to isolate the French, keeping their armies immobile. He had not been able to conclude a pact with Britain, whose policy it was to keep out of any alliances with the countries on the Continent, but he had its friendship. Wilhelm II, however, had perhaps an even stronger Germany than Bismarck's. Certainly its army and navy were stronger than those under Bismarck. He had managed to maintain Germany's alliance with Austria and Italy, the Triple Alliance, but he had killed the treaty with Russia and had never succeeded in dampening the passionate desire of the French to revenge their 1870–71 defeat by the Prussians and reclaim their lost territories, Alsace and Lorraine. And in short order he had so antagonized the British and the Russians that he could truthfully say that Germany was encircled by its enemies.

The policies of Wilhelm II, while perhaps not very different from the policies of the other European powers, were such that war in Europe was sooner or later inevitable; and, murder in Sarajevo or no, in temper and spirit the German people were thoroughly indoctrinated to and prepared for Armageddon.

Triple Entente 4

FOLLOWING Napoleon's defeat and the Congress of Vienna in 1815, British foreign policy called for a "splendid isolation" from the conflicts which occupied the Continent incessantly, and it maintained that policy fairly consistently until the end of the nineteenth century. Only during the 1870–71 Franco-Prussian War did it break precedent, announcing that it was prepared to send its forces against either France or Prussia should either country violate Belgian neutrality, a neutrality which had been pledged by every major power in Europe, including Prussia, in the Treaty of 1839. The swaggering belligerence of Germany's Wilhelm II, however, called for a change in the thinking of the British foreign office. The policy which had kept Britain free of any Continental commitments had to go, and it did, but slowly. It was France which took the first steps toward organizing a bloc of opposition to the Triple Alliance of Germany, Austria, Italy, and later Rumania: a Triple Entente (agreement of friendship), which was to be comprised of France, Russia, and, eventually, Britain.

Even before Wilhelm II took the throne of Germany, the Germans, who had been Russia's chief bankers, made it almost impossible for the Russians to secure loans from their erstwhile friends. Bismarck, in one of his rare errors, thought he was putting pressure on Russia for action favorable to German interests in the Baltic states; instead, he drove the Russians to Paris for the funds they needed badly; France, eager for friendship anywhere on the Continent, was glad to oblige.

In 1890, Wilhelm II did not deem it essential to renew the Three Emperors' Treaty, which bound Russia to Germany and Austria, and he allowed it to lapse. The French seized on the opportunity to develop its incipient good relationship with the Russian government, but the negotiations for some kind of written agreement between the two countries were very slow in materializing.

France, which had been successfully isolated by Bismarck's brilliant diplomacy, and which was having considerable difficulty with Britain in its colonial struggles, was almost desperate for a European ally, but czarist Russia was possessed with an antipathy for the republicanism of France; nor did the French people look kindly on the despotism of the autocracy of Russia. Still, Alexander III, czar of all the Russias, stood at attention to the playing of the Marseillaise, France's revolutionary anthem, when a French squadron pulled in for a visit at Russia's naval base, Kronstadt, in 1891; and in a month, the first of the Franco-Russian agreements was signed.

It was a limited agreement. The two countries would "confer on every question of a nature to threaten the general peace." Further, if either nation were threatened by aggression, they would come to an understanding "on measures which the realization of that eventuality would make it necessary for both governments to adopt immediately and simultaneously." While vague and rather limited, it was an initial step. It was to take another year to work out a hard-core and binding treaty between the two countries.

In August 1892, representatives of the Russians and the French initialed a pact which stipulated that (1) if France were attacked by Germany, or by Italy supported by the Germans, Russia would send seven hundred thousand to eight hundred thousand men to the assistance of the French; and (2) if Russia were attacked by Germany, or Austria supported by Germany, France would put 1.3 million men in the field against the aggressor.

It was not until January 4, 1894, that the French and the Russian governments put their final signatures to the agreement, but France was no longer alone on the European continent. The Triple Entente was in the making.

The full text of the Franco-Russian pact was not available (in fact it was secret), but Wilhelm II must have acquired knowledge of at least its substance. He wrote a "Dear Nicky" letter to his cousin (Britain's Queen Victoria was Wilhelm's grandmother; Nicholas II, czar of Russia, had married a granddaughter of Victoria's). "We Christian Kings and Emperors," he wrote, "have one holy duty, imposed on us by Heaven, that is to uphold the principle of 'By the Grace of God' we can have good relations with the French Republic, but we can never be *intime* (intimate) with her."

It was a high-flown attempt to split the Russians from the French; it did not work. The Franco-Russian pact held.

It was somewhat more difficult for France to develop an agreement with Britain. The British and the French had been traditional enemies over the centuries. Britain had looked with abhorrence on the French Revolution, had fought against Napoleon and defeated him at Waterloo. But it was principally in the struggle for colonies, from America to Asia, where the enmity had been most evident in recent years. Most recently their differences had occurred in Egypt, Morocco, and Newfoundland.

Lord Kitchener, leading a force of British and Egyptian troops, had defeated a French and Ethiopian army at Fashoda in the upper course of the Nile and had entered southern Sudan, claiming it as part of Egypt. The French foreign minister, Théophile Delcassé, yielded to the claim and was glad to accept part of the Sahara in return. He wanted no war with Britain; on the contrary, he was working for some kind of detente with his neighbor across the English Channel. This was in 1899.

In 1904, in a secret treaty, the problem of Morocco was momentarily settled. The treaty gave the British a free hand in all of Egypt, while splitting up Morocco between France and Spain.

The major differences between the French and the British were now cleared up. They could sign an agreement of friendship. That's all it was in 1904—a pact between the two countries which called on them to approach with amity whatever problems they had. It was certainly not a military alliance or an agreement to provide assistance in the event of aggression; still, it was the second leg of a developing Triple Entente and the encirclement of Germany.

It was time for Kaiser Wilhelm II to act, or else it would be too late.

In 1905 the French asked the sultan of Morocco to put his country under the protection of France. This meant a French military presence, French control, everything but French possession of the country. Wilhelm

II responded by sailing his royal yacht into Tangiers and debarking from his boat to declare that Germany was prepared to defend Morocco's independence. He followed by insisting on an international conference at Algiers, where he hoped to drive a wedge between the new Franco-British amity. He failed miserably. The British stuck by their allies; French and Spanish interests were untouched; France was granted the right to patrol the Moroccan-Algerian border; France and Spain were given the right to police Morocco. All Wilhelm II was able to salvage was an assurance that German interests in Morocco would be protected.

Later, in 1908, in an action which was no more than harassment of the French, the German consul in Casablanca gave asylum to deserters from the French Foreign Legion. It was a dispute which was settled, without loss of face to the French, in the Hague Tribunal.

In 1911 the German warship *Panther* appeared at the Moroccan port of Agadir, and this might well have been interpreted as a threat of war; but all the belligerence subsided, for the moment anyway, in the treaty of November 4, 1911, in which Germany granted the right of a French protectorate in Morocco in exchange for a strip of French territory in equatorial Africa.

Wilhelm II's one effort to break the impact of the Franco-Russian agreement, after his "Dear Nicky" letters, occurred in 1905. There was a family gathering of royalty at Bjorkoe in Denmark, and Wilhelm managed to get Nicholas, his cousin, on his yacht. There, as if purely in the spirit of cousins, they signed a pact which provided that each would come to the military aid of the other, "with all forces on land and sea," if one or the other was attacked by another European power. It was a pact that would have negated Russia's agreement with France and Germany's agreement with Austria.

But the signed papers of Bjorkoe were simply dismissed and forgotten.

There remained still one leg before the Triple Entente could become a reality, an agreement between the Russians and the British. The pact would be accomplished, but not without difficulty, and not without time.

The British had come to the aid of Turkey and defeated the Russians in the Crimean War of 1854–56. Following the defeat of the Turks by the Russians in another of their innumerable wars, in 1877, Benjamin Disraeli, the British prime minister—and great statesman—sent a fleet into the Dardanelles to save Constantinople, as well as the important sea passage, from the Russians.

In 1902 Britain signed a treaty with Japan, with the obvious intention of putting a rein on Russia's ambitions in Manchuria and China. The Russian defeat in the Russo-Japanese War of 1905 did nothing to heal the breach between Russia and Britain.

But the presence of Wilhelm II on the European scene, particularly his naval challenge to British domination of the seas and his Berlin-to-Bagdad railroad scheme, which threatened Britain's hold in the subcontinent of India, had the effect of softening the British attitude toward Russia. Similarly, the open threat by the Germans of a "preventive war" against France and their intrusion into the Turko-Balkan problems eased Russia's belligerent attitude toward Britain.

In 1907 the two countries came to an understanding, an entente, settling the major difference between them: the Persian dispute, over which both countries had nearly gone to war. The country was neatly divided —without Persian consent at all, of course—Russia gaining control in northern Persia, Britain in southern, with a neutral zone in the center. Tibet was to remain under the dominion of China; Russia and Britain were to move out of the territory; and Afghanistan was to remain under the control of, but not be annexed by, the British.

The Triple Entente was now a complete entity. There was the agreement of friendship between Britain and France, a similar agreement of friendship between Britain and Russia, and a military alliance between Russia and France.

Italy, which was officially a partner in the Triple Alliance with Germany and Austria, in 1902 signed a pact with France in which each country guaranteed its neutrality should the other be attacked by a European power. The pact obviously nullified her obligations to her two Alliance partners. Except for Austria and the rather weak Rumania, Germany stood alone in the center of Europe, surrounded by a France eager to avenge its defeat of 1870 and reclaim its lost provinces; by a Britain which looked with antagonism on the German navy, on German commerce, on German claims to glory; and by the giant of a bear, Russia, sitting on its flanks.

It was essential to Germany that she keep her one ally strong, and her one ally, Austria-Hungary, was having its difficulties with the Balkan Serbian ambitions and with the intensifying Slav nationalist movements in its Balkan provinces.

There was no question in the mind of the German foreign office or its general staff that war between the Triple Alliance (now really "Dual Alliance") and the Triple Entente was inevitable.

In May 1914, General Helmuth von Moltke, chief of staff of the German armies, declared, "We are ready (for war) and the sooner the better for us."

The war was not long in coming. Serbia and the Austro-Hungarian province of Bosnia would soon enough provide the impetus to test the great military might of Wilhelm II's Germany, its vision of conquest, and its dream of glory.

Austria-Hungary and the Serbian Unrest

THE RISING nationalist fevers which made themselves evident in open rebellion in Europe during the second half of the nineteenth century and the first years of the twentieth were the signal for the beginning of the end of the once mighty Austro-Hungarian Empire, and for the House of Hapsburg, which had maintained its power uninterrupted since the early days of the Renaissance. In 1859, the Italian Count Camillo Cavour, in the process of creating a unified Italy with the aid of Napoleon III of France, drove the Austrians out of the Italian peninsula. In 1866, the Prussians' quick defeat of the Hapsburg armies delegated Austria to a second-place position in the Germanic world, the Hapsburgs ceding their leadership of the Germanic people to the Prussians and the newly created German Empire. When the Magyars (not Germans) who peopled Hungary gave evidence of their intention to rebel against Hapsburg domination, to separate Hungary from the empire as an independent state—just one year after the disastrous war with the Prussians—Franz Josef, emperor of Austria-Hungary, managed to smooth the rebellious spirits with a compromise. Austria and Hungary were declared separate and sovereign states, each with its own government and parliament. However, there was to be one ruler, titled Emperor of Austria and King of Hungary. And there was to be a three-member common cabinet to conduct the financial and foreign affairs of both states and to tend to their common defense. It was an arrangement which worked well for more than fifty years, until the final dissolution of the empire.

But, for all Austria-Hungary's setbacks and defeats, its rulers were not prepared to retire in the shadow of the other great powers in Europe. Thwarted and routed in the west, the Hapsburgs turned to the east and the south. They began to probe the Balkans, which were the outright properties, or vassal states, of the Ottoman Empire (Turkey). The Ottoman Empire was no longer the mighty force it once had been, when its domain stretched out from Asia and into Europe. It had lost territory to Russia and even to its vassal Balkan states, which it held only by the strength of its arms and its frequently brutal and bloody administration. It was known by its well-earned title, "the sick man of Europe," and whatever holdings it had left in the European continent could have been quickly gobbled up, particularly by the Russians, were it not for the threat of French and English, as well as Austrian, intervention.

At the Congress of Berlin, called to check Russian aggrandizement, the Europeans did a little carving up of Turkey's possessions on their own. Serbia and Rumania were given full independence from the Ottoman Empire, the British got Cyprus, and Austria-Hungary was granted full control, political and military, over the Balkan's largely Slav-populated provinces of Bosnia and Hercegovina.

This was a pleasant change in the Austro-Hungarian fortunes, and they lost no time at all capitalizing on it. Before the end of July, 1878, they had sent four divisions of troops under General Josef Philipovic von Philipsberg to take over their easily won prize.

The Catholics of the provinces greeted the Catholic troops of the Catholic emperor with open arms as they marched across their frontiers into Bosnia-Hercegovina. This was the one peaceful gesture in the Hapsburg takeover. The rest was resistance and bloodshed.

The Serbs, who were of the Orthodox Church, had settled in Bosnia-Hercegovina sometime in the seventh century, but had lived under Turkish rule and domination since 1463. They were glad enough to be freed from the fist of the Ottoman Empire, but their dream was a unification with Serbia and not the Austrian Empire. They viewed the entering Hapsburg troops with suspicion and hostility.

It was the Moslem population (some thirty percent of the inhabitants of the provinces), roused by their religious leaders, who took to arms against the invaders.

The Catholic Franz Josef, they were led to believe, meant to destroy their mosques, their houses of worship; and the Moslems attacked and defended, making the Austrians pay heavily for what the Moslems considered their land.

From the moment the four Hapsburg divisions—three from the north and one from the west—crossed from Austria into Bosnia-Hercegovina, they found the going bloody. At Maglaj, they encountered fire from both banks of its river. There was solid resistance and a house-to-house battle before they could take the town. In the area of Tuzla, the fighting was so fierce that the Austrians were forced into a temporary retreat. They burned the town of Brcko to the ground in reprisal for "treacherous" action on the part of the inhabitants.

General Josef Philipovic von Philipsberg had to call for three fresh Hapsburg divisions for his march on Sarajevo, the capital city of Bosnia, which he took only after three weeks of stiff house-to-house resistance. He needed an additional four divisions to send to the provinces where the fighting continued despite the loss of the Bosnians' principal city.

In the northeastern sector of Bosnia, Hapsburg General Szapary was bogged down in two weeks of critical warfare. In the western sections of the province, in the battle of Kljuc, the Austro-Hungarians lost more than three hundred men. There were further heavy losses for the Hapsburg troops in the remote area of Krajina.

It took two hundred thousand Austro-Hungarian troops three months of fighting before Austria-Hungary could pacify the territory the Congress of Berlin had handed it. It took the loss of 5,198 Hapsburg troops (killed, wounded, or missing), 178 of them officers, before Austria-Hungary could claim control of the provinces. The Moslems, who also had suffered heavy losses, were quieted and pacified, but the Serbian and Croat Slavs would never acquiesce to Hapsburg rule; and they were determined to demonstrate dramatically their distaste for the hasty Austro-Hungarian occupation of Bosnia-Hercegovina.

The Congress of Berlin had given control of the two Balkan provinces to the Hapsburgs. Nominally, they still belonged to Turkey; and Serbia, rather unrealistically, believed that the Hapsburgs would eventually cede to them what the Serbians considered a temporary mandate. The Serbs, considering the population of the provinces was seventy percent Croat and Serbian Slav, deemed that the provinces rightfully belonged to them and fully expected that Bosnia-Hercegovina would be incorporated under the Serbian flag in due time.

The Hapsburgs, of course, were of a different opinion. In 1908, having bought off the Russians with a shady promise of Austrian support for a Russian drive toward the Dardanelles, Vienna announced with impunity the annexation of the two provinces, Bosnia and Hercegovina. The Serbians were outraged!

They demanded immediate action from their government. The streets of Belgrade were jammed with mob demonstrations.

"Down with Austria!"

"Death to the Hapsburgs!"

"War!"

The Serbians are a proud people. Volatile, courageous, unafraid of battle, their history is rife with violence. Petar Karadjordjevic, chief of state of the semi-autonomous Serbia, was assassinated in 1812. Milosh Obrenovic, who had arranged the assassination and had replaced Karadjordjevic, was forced into exile, and the son of Petar Karadjordjevic, Alexander, was recalled to head the state. Milosh, in turn, returned to Serbia with his son Michael, ousted the son of Karadjordjevic and placed his own son on the throne. Michael Obrenovic was eventually murdered, and his cousin, Prince Milam, became Serbia's king.

Milam, in 1881, signed a secret ten-year pact with the Austrians, which was to lead to his downfall. According to the terms of the pact, Serbia would not commit itself to any other political treaty without the consent of the Hapsburgs, and it pledged itself to prevent any "political or religious agitation" directed against Austria-Hungary within its province. Austria-Hungary, for its part, made a pledge to support Serbian ambitions for expansion. It was a pact which, in effect, placed Serbia in a position of subservience to the Hapsburg Empire.

The agreement, of course, could not be kept completely secret, and the hostile reaction might well have been expected. In the following year an attempt to assassinate Milam failed, but in 1889 he was forced to abdicate in favor of his thirteen-year-old son Alexander.

Alexander was scarcely an improvement on his father. Only four years after he assumed leadership of the kingdom, both he and his wife, Draga—a woman considerably older than he was, and reputedly of loose morals—were brutally assassinated. They were shot, hacked, and thrown out of their palace windows.

Lieutenant Dragutin Dimitrijevic, an extraordinarily powerful young man (nicknamed Apis after the bull-god of ancient Egypt), was one of the leaders of the young officers responsible for the assassination, and was wounded in the battle around the palace. It was Apis who was to play a central role, later, in the assassination in Sarajevo.

The turbulence and violence of Serbia took another direction in the years 1912 and 1913. In March 1912 Serbia signed a secret treaty with Bulgaria; in September it signed a secret treaty with Montenegro. In May of that year, Bulgaria and Greece put their signatures to a secret treaty. All three treaties, in substance, carried the same provisions.

First, the three countries agreed to a mutual military assistance to prevent the efforts of any great power, or powers, to annex what was still Turkish Balkan territory.

Second, they agreed that either signatory (to any of the three pacts) could initiate a proposal for an attack on Turkey; that if there were a lack of agreement on this issue, the question would be put to Russia, giving Russia the power to make the binding decision.

Third, making their intentions clear, they divided among themselves the lands of the Ottoman Empire that they were to "liberate" and annex.

The First Balkan War followed almost immediately, and by May 1913 the combined forces of the Serbs, the Bulgars, the Montenegrins, and the Greeks had driven the Turks almost completely out of Europe. The Ottoman Empire was forced to relinquish all its European territory except for Constantinople and the thin strip of land around it. Everything might have ended in a satisfactory manner in the Balkans, and there might have been peace, but Austria-Hungary stepped into the negotiations which followed the war, primarily because it did not enjoy the prospect of a strong Serbia on its Bosnia-Hercegovina borders. The Pan-Slavic movement, the movement to unite all the Slavs under the one Serbian monarchy, was powerful in Serbia, and the annexation of Bosnia and Hercegovina was one of its prime targets.

As a result of the intervention of the Hapsburgs, who insisted on the creation of an independent state for the Balkan Albanians, Serbia was forced to relinquish territory which her secret pacts had assigned her. To make up for the loss, the Serbs asked for a readjustment of their claims in Macedonia. This would have required Bulgaria to give up some of the territory it had been allotted in the three pacts, which it refused to do. Instead, overestimating its military strength, Bulgaria attacked its erstwhile allies, with disastrous results.

Serbia and Greece, aided by Rumania, as well as by the Turks, who were glad for the opportunity to avenge their defeat at least on the Bulgars, routed the forces of Bulgaria, which was forced to surrender much that it had gained in the first of the Balkan wars.

With Serbia's two victories, in 1912 and 1913, national pride soared. Its dream of a greater Serbia grew. It looked to the west, and the agitation—however muted for diplomatic and military reasons—for annexation of the Hapsburg-held, largely Slav-populated provinces of Bosnia and Hercegovina became increasingly evident. The echoes of the Serbian victories were heard plainly enough by the Austrians, and by the Germans, who were quick to send General Liman von Sanders to reorganize (really, to control) the Turkish army. But it was in Bosnia-Hercegovina that the impact of Serbian victory was to become most dramatically evident. For a long time there had been both open and secret agitation for the liberation of Bosnia and Hercegovina from Hapsburg rule, for the provinces to join their brother and sister Slavs under the Serbian banner. The Serbian conquests gave a drive to that agitation, quickening its pace. Terror and violence were its ultimate results.

The Secret Societies 6

On October 8, 1908—two days after Austria-Hungary announced its annexation of Bosnia and Hercegovina—a group of Serb nationalists, soldiers, and civilians, met to organize the secret society *Narodna Odbrana* (National Defense). It was a meeting attended by Milovan Milovanovic, the Serbian foreign minister, and by other ministers and army officers high in the Serbian ranks. Its first president was the elderly and hardly radical Serbian general, Boza Jankosic. The program of the organization called for the enlistment and the training of secret volunteers for an envisioned war against the Hapsburg monarchy, to enlist a corps of spies and saboteurs to be employed in the Slav territories held by the Austro-Hungarian Empire, and to carry on an organized campaign of propaganda both at home and abroad against the Hapsburg regime, wherever it existed.

Its work was well planned and effective. Within a very short time, its agents were operating throughout Bosnia, and the results of its efforts, its smuggling of arms, propaganda, and agents from Belgrade to Sarajevo prompted Austria to take stern action. Early in 1909, the *Narodna Odbrana* had done so well with its program that the Hapsburgs demanded that Serbia put an end to its activities. The implied threat of invasion in the note from Vienna forced the *Narodna Odbrana* to curtail some of its more violent anti-Austrian propaganda, since Serbia alone could scarcely expect to stop a Hapsburg onslaught, and the Russians, at the moment, were a little too friendly with the Austro-Hungarians.

However, the *Narodna Odbrana* did not disband. It continued its propaganda in its native Serbia and soon gave birth to another and far more violent and dangerous secret organization.

Secret organizations were not new to the Serbians. As early as the 1830s, Prince Adam Jerzy Czartoryski, who had emigrated to France with so many others of his countrymen with the crushing of the Polish rebellion of 1830–31, had a corps of secret agents in every Balkan country. Serbia, he wrote, was the country which would lead and incorporate all southern Slavs into one nation.

Ilija Garasanin, a Serbian statesman when Serbia was still a vassal state, built a string of secret societies, mainly in Bosnia and Hercegovina. The purpose of the societies was to gather information, military and civil, and to pass this information on to the Serbian government, the better to prepare Serbia for a projected invasion and liberation of the provinces.

In the 1860s a number of secret societies were organized by southern Slav students in the different university centers of Europe. In 1866 the secret organization of young men at the university in Vienna sent out a call to sixteen similar societies in Austria-Hungary, Serbia, and other European countries to attend a joint conference; its purpose was the creation of an organization to be named "United Serbian Youth."

Officially, the United Serbian Youth was an educational society. Unofficially, it contained a number of secret groups devoted to tasks the Hapsburgs considered revolutionary: the liberation of Balkan territory from the Austro-Hungarian Empire and the creation of the Slav state of Greater Serbia. Although branches of the United Serbian Youth were established wherever a south Slav population existed, the organization, except for its secret elements, ceased to function effectively in a relatively short time.

Toward the end of the century high school boys in Bosnia, Hercegovina, other south Slav states and provinces, and even in Austria-Hungary began organizing secret and sometimes revolutionary societies. Never organized into a single unit with a written constitution and a written program, they became known collectively as the Young Bosnians. As might have been expected, their interests and their concepts of south Slav problems varied, as did their ideas concerning the solution of those problems.

Dimitrije Mitrinovic of Hercegovina was instrumental in creating a secret library in Mostar, the capital of the province, in 1904. It was this sixteen-year-old schoolboy's conviction that liberation and unity among the south Slavs could be wrought out of a development of south Slav culture. The library was kept secret because of official censorship which prohibited the reading of "revolutionary" material, and because of the presence of anarchist, nihilist and socialist books and pamphlets which were smuggled into the provinces.

Sloboda (Freedom) was another schoolboy organization which appeared at the time. Its leader was Bogdan Zerajic, who would later attempt the assassination of the Austrian governor of Bosnia, General Marijan Varesanin, then kill himself with the last bullet in his gun. *Sloboda* considered itself ultra-Serbian nationalist, but still its members attended Mitrinovic's secret meetings, while members of the secret library organization attended meetings of *Sloboda*. There was an undeclared unity among all the Young Bosnian secret societies; each in its own way openly challenged the authority of the state, the church, the school; and wherever a Young Bosnian group existed—in Serbia, in Montenegro, in Bosnia-Hercegovina, in Austria-Hungary itself, and even among the south Slavs who had emigrated to the United States—the goal was the destruction of the Austro-Hungarian Empire and the unification of the south Slavs into a single nation.

When the Hapsburgs annexed Bosnia and Hercegovina, the reaction of the Young Bosnian schoolboys was violent. Some fled from the territory to Montenegro and Serbia; some, hoping for Serbian intervention, enlisted in the Serbian army. At the university in Vienna, where young Bosnians had been joined in a cultural society called *Rad* (Work), they organized a secret society whose declared aim was to struggle against Austro-Hungarian domination. They announced, in their manifesto, that they would never recognize the Hapsburg takeover of Bosnia and Hercegovina, and a number of them returned to Serbia to receive training in partisan and guerrilla tactics from their comrades in the *Narodna Odbrana*.

Dimitrije Mitrinovic was one of the six organizers of this Vienna group. He had come under the influence of the more revolutionary students at the university, where he was then studying, and had moved a considerable distance from his secret library days. He headed a secret band of three, as did the five other original members of the secret order. None of the "members of three" was aware of the identity of any of the other groups of three. The entire organization, as it expanded into Sarajevo and the various other districts of Bosnia-Hercegovina, was carefully constructed to protect against the possibility of Austrian police penetration into its ranks, or the betrayal by a backslider. Should one of its members be apprehended by the Austrian authorities, he could deliver to the enemy, at most, the names of only two others in the organization. Nor were the rules and regulations of this secret society ever put down on paper; nor did they ever record the minutes of their separate meetings. Any communication among the groups of three was written in code. Utmost secrecy was essential to the struggle against the Hapsburgs, their army, and their police, and the method of organization of the groups of three was adopted by other Young Bosnians, as well as by other militant groups.

In Sarajevo, meanwhile, the Austrian authorities put a ban on any student literary, political, or athletic organization, except for the Saint Mary Congregation, headed by a Jesuit priest; they also prohibited students from joining any public societies, as guest or member, under threat of expulsion from their classes. But even as the authorities were setting down these bans, Danilo Ilic, a writer and teacher, was busy organizing the younger students at the high schools into the Young Bosnians and the secret societies. The young men not only were outraged by the Hapsburg ban on their civil liberties; they also were irate with the immorality displayed by the Austrians, claiming that the Hapsburgs intended to destroy the moral fiber of the Slavs, and so their ability to shake off the Austro-Hungarian shackles.

The Young Bosnians, or at least the great majority of them, were puritanical in spirit, and in action as well. They were ascetics. Their organizations called for an obligatory abstinence from lovemaking and drinking. Bogdan Zerajic was twenty-five years old when he put a bullet into his head after his attempted assassination of the Bosnian governor, but he had never made love to a woman. Similarly, Gavrilo Princip, the main figure in the Sarajevo assassination, never made physical love to a woman; nor did he ever drink even so much as wine until he began to sit at the tables of the Sarajevo cafes in his effort to mislead the Austrian police.

It is impossible to know just how many young schoolboys joined the Young Bosnians when the Hapsburgs set up special military brothels in Sarajevo; but the Hapsburg gesture certainly stiffened the backs and the will of the young rebels.

Danilo Ilic was to prove an important link between these younger Young Bosnians and the movement's more mature members in the preparations for the assassination in Sarajevo.

There were other secret societies. Serb and Croat students organized a joint secret organization which, among other points in its program, called for "radical elimination of destructive alien influence, and promotion of Slavization of our culture against Germanization, Magyarization and Italianization." Slovenes organized a secret society they named *Preporod* (Rebirth) and called for a revolutionary destruction of the Austro-Hungarian Empire. None of the secret organizations, however, had the impact of the secret *Ujedinjenje ili Smrt* (Union or Death), better known as the *Crna ruka* (Black Hand), which grew out of the *Narodna Odbrana*, under the leadership of Colonel Dragutin Dimitrijevic, the army officer who had been wounded in the assassination of King Alexander and his wife Draga.

It was the Black Hand which would assign the target for assassination in Sarajevo and select, train, and prepare the young assassins for its successful conclusion.

The Black Hand   7

UNTIL the Hapsburg annexation of Bosnia-Hercegovina and the events which quickly followed, Colonel Dragutin Dimitrijevic (Apis) had been primarily an
army man. He had no particular interest in party politics, nor was he especially interested in Serbia's foreign
policy. He was concerned, however, with the chief of
state, and how his country was governed.

At the age of twenty-four, as a young lieutenant, he
had been one of the leading organizers, perhaps the
main organizer, of the first attempt to assassinate a cor-
rupt and autocratic King Alexander and his queen. It
was a bungled affair. The plan had first called for an
attack on the Belgrade power plants to cut the elec-
tricity; at that precise moment, the conspirators, in attendance at a ball given in honor of the queen, were to
set fire to the hall, sound the alarm, and in the confusion
poison the king and his wife.

It was amateurishly conceived and amateurishly executed. The cabal had even tested the poison on a cat;
the poison worked, but the rest did not. Apis's men
couldn't take the electric plants; they were too well
guarded. And the king and queen had neglected to
attend the party.

This was in 1901. In 1902, an undiscouraged Apis

persuaded a number of officers to take an oath dedicating themselves to the regicide:

"In anticipation of the collapse of the state if the existing conditions continue for even the shortest time, and blaming for this primarily the King and his paramour Draga, we swear that we shall murder them and to that effect affix our signatures."

A year later, in June 1903, the murders were carried out. A group of young army officers stormed the palace, discovered the king and queen hiding behind a secret door in their bedroom, shot them, butchered them, and tossed them, naked, bleeding, and dead, out of the palace windows.

There were others marked for death on the night of the regicide; they were routed out—from the cafes, from their homes—and killed.

Apis was badly wounded by the gunfire of the palace guards—he would carry three bullets in his body until his death some fourteen years later—but he had won himself a key position in the history of Serbia. In Belgrade, he was called "the savior of the fatherland," but if Apis enjoyed this new prestige, he did not demonstrate it. Whenever he spoke of the palace coup of 1903, he talked only of the bravery of his comrades, never of his own participation in the raid and the assassination. His actions had been those of an army officer; he had done only that which he had considered his military duty; at least, this is how he wanted his action evaluated.

With the Bosnia-Hercegovina annexation, however, there came a change in the tactics of Apis. He was forced to look beyond his limited, army-oriented interests to examine and assess the activities of the ministers in the parliament of his country, their foreign policy, and the effect of this policy on the life of his people. His new direction of inquiry and action brought him into direct conflict with the Serbian politicos, and particularly with the Serbian prime minister, Nikola Pasic. Pasic was the leader of the Radical Party, a party which had become radical in name only, and which had been moving more and more to the right of center. The young Serbian liberals and radicals, particularly the zealous Slav nationalists, made Pasic one of their favorite targets. However, the attack of Apis on the prime minister was more subtle, and perhaps more dangerous to the political life of an aging but still very shrewd and capable Pasic.

The influence of army men on the political lives of their countries was a phenomenon common to the time, the early 1900s. In every sovereign state of Europe there was a rapid growth in the size of armies, a rapidly rising budget for armaments, and a military which was fast becoming an independent force with a growing impact on governmental decisions, both in domestic programs and in foreign diplomacy and action. Apis was in step with his times.

At the time of the successful 1903 palace coup, Apis —who was only twenty-six years old—might well have assumed the top post in the Serbian army. He did not. He might have had himself named minister of war— and in fact it was common knowledge that he administered that branch of the Serbian government—but he never officially took the post. Apis was a man who preferred to work behind the scenes, to be the man behind the king, the kingmaker. He was a conspirator by nature; not ambitious for rank or title, he did little if anything to advance his own position, but was always prodding his friends, and helping them, to climb the ladder of whatever dream they imagined for themselves. He won friendships easily and held on to them, a trait so essential for leadership in the art of conspiracy. An evenness of temper and a control in speech and action were other characteristics of this man, who was perhaps the arch-conspirator, the arch-regicide of his times.

And he was courageous, as he demonstrated in the palace attack. He was unable to participate as a fighting soldier in the First Balkan War, against Turkey, but he moved, disguised, into Ottoman territory and persuaded the Albanians, still under Turkish rule, to lend their aid to the Serbian cause.

Apis paid for his raid into the Ottoman Empire by contracting a rare disease, Maltese fever. It was an illness from which he recovered slowly and which prevented him from taking an active command of Serbian troops. In 1913 he was assigned, or more likely had himself assigned, to the Serbian general staff as chief of its intelligence division. It was a post which would serve him well in the powerful and secret terrorist organization which he would help create and lead—the feared Black Hand.

There were numbers of civilians involved in the planning stages of this ultranationalist secret society, principally the revolutionary Ljuba Jovanovic. Jovanovic had worked as a servant to support himself while he was in secondary school. When he enrolled in the Belgrade Law School, he helped organize the *Slovenski Jug,* a group which advocated unification of all south Slavs by revolutionary methods. He was active in the street demonstrations organized by students in 1903. He had fought against the Turkish armies in Macedonia. He was undoubtedly a fit companion for Apis and his conspiracy, though it would be some time before the two men met in a common cause.

Beginning in the spring of 1909 and into the fall of that year, Jovanovic met with different groups of men who, with him, believed Serbia was ready for a revolutionary, patriotic, secret society. Several of these sessions were held outside of Belgrade, at least one of them in Brussels. Bogdan Radenkovic, who in 1910 was to become an official with the ministry of foreign affairs, attended several of the meetings. Radenkovic had at one time been sentenced to death by the Turks for his efforts to free his Slav brothers from Turkish rule. Petar Zivkovic, a general in the Serbian army, who had opened the gates of the palace in the 1903 assassination, was another who met with the cabal. Also attending the meetings were Major Milan Pribicevic, once an officer in the Hapsburg armies, but now in exile because of his revolutionary activities; and Major Vojin Tankosic, who was to play a key role in the assassination of Franz Ferdinand in Sarajevo.

Apis was mentioned time and again at these clandestine sessions, but he was not approached, according to certain stories, until March 6, 1911. It would seem, however, that Apis, with his broad and efficient espionage system, had been aware of the work of this group of nationalists from its beginning.

In any case, Apis gave no indication of his pre-knowledge as the ideas of the conspirators were explained to him. He listened politely and attentively, as he always did. When asked whether he would join with the cabal, there was no hesitation on his part. He accepted the invitation on principle, but he wanted a hand in the final formulation of its constitution, its oath, and its program.

Within two months, on May 9, 1911, ten conspirators, army men and civilians, met to adopt the constitution of the new secret organization. They called it *Ujedinjenje ili Smrt* (Union or Death). Its enemies, those who feared it, would call it the Black Hand.

Its first president was Colonel Ilija Radivojevic, the

man who, with Velimir Nemic, another of the organizers of the Black Hand, had been the actual assassins in the 1903 coup. But it was Apis, choosing as usual to remain out of the limelight, who was the actual leader of the cabal from its beginning as a terrorist organization.

The Black Hand had been a long time in its planning process. Considerable pains had been taken to spell out its purpose and program with precision. Its constitution left nothing to the imagination, or to interpretation. Its wording was exact.

Its first article began: "This organization is formed in order to achieve the ideal of unification of Serbdom; all Serbs, regardless of sex, religion or place of birth, can become members, and anyone else who is prepared to serve this ideal faithfully."

Article two defined the manner in which the society was to operate: "This organization chooses revolutionary [terrorist] action . . . and is therefore secret. . . ."

In other articles, the constitution declared that the Black Hand would organize "revolutionary activities in all territories inhabited by Serbs" and would "fight with all means available those outside its [Serbia's] frontiers who are enemies" of the unification of all Serbs.

With Apis as its leader, the Black Hand felt certain that it would not be remiss in carrying forward its program.

Each of the organizers of the terrorist group signed his own name to the society's constitution. The rest was utter secrecy. The recruits—in blocks of three, four, and five, with each cell headed by a member of the society's central committee—used aliases. Except for the central committee, individual members were identified only by a given number. This kind of secrecy was extremely important, of course, considering the number of its members who were high in the seats of government and in the ranks of the army (Apis, for example, was with the Serbian general staff). But despite the presence of such prominent men, the manner in which it initiated new members into the society was almost schoolboyishly melodramatic.

The initiate was led into a darkened room by a member of the organization, who lit a candle on a small table; on the table, covered by a black cloth, were a carefully placed dagger and revolver and a cross. The intentions of the Black Hand, its purpose and goal, were thoroughly explained to the initiate for the second and perhaps third time; and then, in utter silence, the door to the room opened for a man in a black cloak, a black hood, and a black mask. The man in black walked to the other side of the table. He said nothing. He stood still, motionless.

"I [name of the initiate]," began the member who had led the initiate into the darkened room, "becoming a member of the organization *Ujedinjenje ili Smrt . . .*"

The member of the Black Hand waited for the initiate to repeat the words, the beginning of his oath of membership, then went on, pausing after each phrase for the repetition by the initiate.

". . . swear by the sun which is shining on me, by the earth which is feeding me, by God, by the blood of my ancestors, by my honor and my life, that from this moment until my death, I will serve faithfully the cause of this organization and will always be ready to undergo sacrifices for it. . . ."

The initiate swore to carry out all the commands of the Black Hand "unconditionally" and to take all its secrets "to the grave."

The oath of allegiance administered, the man who had led the initiate into the darkened room embraced him. The mysterious man in black, actually a member of the executive committee of the Black Hand, shook the initiate's hand, maintaining his silence, and walked out.

The lights in the room were then turned on, the constitution and the bylaws of the secret organization read to the initiate, who then signed his name to the written oath he had taken. The Black Hand had added a new name (or, rather, a new number) to its rolls.

The actual number of members enrolled in the Black Hand has never been firmly determined; there was too much well-kept secrecy for that. But its membership grew at a rapid pace, and by 1914 there were, conservatively, some twenty-five hundred army officers, lawyers, journalists, members of the government, university professors, and even schoolboys who had taken its oath of allegience.

Members of the Black Hand were sent to infiltrate other secret organizations, clubs, and societies. They operated within the *Narodna Odbrana*, infiltrating its central committee as well as its local chapters. It moved into the Young Bosnian groups and was effective in influencing their decisions and their activities. They were assigned, probably by direction of Apis, to a number of key border posts, on both the Turkish and the Austrian borders, where they served in a dual capacity: they were responsible for the free passage of men, arms, and propaganda out of Serbia to their comrades in the Ottoman Empire, Bosnia, Hercegovina, other Slav territories, and Vienna itself; and they acted as revolutionary agents, fomenting and developing anti-Hapsburg activities in the areas to which they had been assigned. In addition, they proved the means for gathering information and passing it on to the Black Hand headquarters. The Russian military attaché in Belgrade at the time, Colonel Victor Artamonov, sponsored this last activity in part, giving Apis sums of money from time to time to support his program. Much was made of this Russian aid later in the investigation of the assassination in Sarajevo; but it is doubtful that the Russians were aware of the terrorist program of the Black Hand, or even of the connection between Apis and the secret society.

Among its other activities, the Black Hand also set up a school for guerrilla fighting, where the fine arts of espionage (firing a pistol, bomb-throwing, bridge destruction) were diligently taught, primarily to the young people of ultranationalistic persuasion.

It is not certain, but most likely it was the Black Hand which was responsible for the aborted attempt on the life of the emperor of Austria-Hungary, Franz Josef, in 1911, as well as the unsuccessful effort at assassinating the Austrian governor of Croatia.

The Serbian government, of course, was not unaware of the Black Hand activities. If Nikola Pasic did not know for certain that Apis headed the organization, he must have suspected it strongly. The battle lines between the civilian forces on one hand, the army forces on the other, for control of Serbian foreign policy, had been growing sharper, more easily defined. While Pasic was still in control, that control had been loosened considerably, and there could be no doubt that Apis and his Black Hand constituted the chief threat to continued civilian authority. Still, there was little that Nikola Pasic, artful diplomat that he was, could do to stem the waxing power of either the Black Hand or its leader. Certainly, he was practically powerless to block the Black Hand's decision to make its most crucial action, the assassination of the Archduke Franz Ferdinand in Sarajevo, on the twenty-eighth of June, 1914.

The Plot

8

THERE have been shelves of books and pamphlets written on just when and where and how the plot to assassinate Archduke Franz Ferdinand originated, how it was organized, and how the assassination was accomplished. The testimony of the assassins and their alleged associates at the hearings and trials which followed the political murder was often contradictory; there was a tendency on the part of some—an actual rivalry between two of them, Nedeljko Cabrinovic and Gavrilo Princip—to claim the principal role in both planning and executing the assassination. Undoubtedly, an element of pride, as well as the ardent desire to play the martyr, a wish common to not a few young Bosnian nationalists, lent itself to considerable exaggeration in the evidence they gave at their inquiries and trials. There was also need to protect those in high government posts, as well as those accomplices not apprehended, and this certainly must have colored their testimony; and there is no doubt that ranking officers and perhaps government officials were involved in the plot.

Among the various studies and theories developed on the Sarajevo assassination, there were several suggestions, even accusations, of international involvements.

This is an area of investigation which cannot be completed until all the relevant archives of some of Europe's greater powers have been opened. Nor can the accusations, most of them politically motivated, be entirely dismissed, particularly when the espionage activities of Colonel Dragutin Dimitrijevic—Apis, leader of the Black Hand—are considered.

Colonel Victor Artamonov, the Russian military attaché in Belgrade, had supplied Apis with money for espionage in Austria-Hungary; and imperial Russia was Austria's rival for control of the Balkans. There was the Russian Pan-Slavic movement, which influenced the nationalist thinking and action of the Serbs. In addition, the Young Bosnians had been considerably affected by the teachings of Russian anarchists and social revolutionaries, who believed in and employed terrorist activities.

In Hungary, the Magyars had a completely outspoken antipathy for the Slavs of any nation. The Hungarian prime minister, Count Stephen Tisza, had been the chief opponent in the Austro-Hungarian Empire to the annexation of Bosnia and Hercegovina. He had also been a vehement spokesman against the idea of Trialism, the creation of an Austro-Hungarian-Slav Empire which would have included the southern Slavs in a separate and autonomous state. Archduke Franz Ferdinand was a leading advocate of Trialism, and Tisza dreaded the day he would assume the throne of the Hapsburgs. It has been suggested by several historians that there was an association between Count Tisza and Apis—an association that may have had a bearing on the Sarajevo killings.

There were strong anti-Hapsburg elements in Germany, too. The dream of a greater Germany, which began with Bismarck, envisioned the inclusion of all

Germanic people—and the people of Austria were German. Obviously, the end of the Hapsburgs would make the accomplishment of such a dream more feasible. Maximilian Hohenberg, the son of Archduke Franz Ferdinand, was one of those who accused the Germans of being involved with Apis in the assassination of his mother and father.

Nor were the French and British spared accusation of complicity in the Sarajevo murders. The charges against France and Britain emanated from Germany, eager to escape the onus of having started the war which engulfed Europe almost immediately after the assassination. It was, the Germans concluded, the British and the French intelligence services which had arranged the murder of the archduke to establish an excuse for an attack on the German Empire.

The Germans, and certain Catholic elements, also accused the Freemasons of plotting to kill, and killing, the heir to the Austro-Hungarian throne. Franz Ferdinand was an ardently devout Catholic. International Freemasonry was the avowed enemy of the Jesuits.

The Germans also accused the Jews of being involved in the assassination. Gavrilo Princip, the young Bosnian whose bullets killed the archduke and his wife, was accused of being both a Freemason and a Jew (he was neither).

Princip came from Bosnian peasant stock. He was the fourth child and the second son of a letter-carrier, Petar. There were nine children born to the family, but only three survived their infancy. Gavrilo was born July 13, 1894, according to the testimony given at his trial; June 13, 1894, according to the civil registry. The date was going to have a bearing on the sentence he would receive for the murders; a matter of fifteen days would save him from being hanged by the neck until he was dead.

Gavrilo Princip was a slight, lean young man, blue-eyed and curly-haired, with a pointed chin—an earnest young man, more given to reading, to study, to memorizing his favorite poets, than to the social life of the young people around him. Even as a boy, before he could be enrolled, he played at going to school, carrying some old books in a knapsack on his back. He was a loner and, probably because of his size (he was always small for his years), he was pugnacious, quick to retaliate when he was attacked and unafraid to take on boys twice as big as he was. He was to be rejected, however, by the army when he made an effort to enlist with the Serbians, because he was considered too lean, too small, too weak. He may have been physically weak; he made up for that deficiency with a rather belligerent will, a fierce determination, and pride.

He wanted to go to school and, at the age of nine, despite the opposition of his father, who needed the young boy to watch the family's small flock of sheep, he began his primary education in a school some two miles from where he lived in the Grahovo Valley. The small schoolhouse was the beginning of his rather checkered education.

When he was thirteen, Gavrilo Princip left his native village and traveled to Sarajevo, where, with the financial aid of his older brother Jovo, he enrolled in the Merchants School. Jovo also found him his lodgings, a room in the house of Stoja Ilic, a widow who lived alone with her son. Her son was Danilo Ilic, who, as Jovo Princip could not possibly have known, was an ardent Young Bosnian activist. Ilic, his library of nationalist and revolutionary books and pamphlets, his talk and his ideas, were to prove key influences in the life of the peasant boy Gavrilo Princip; Ilic would also be a key figure in the Sarajevo assassination.

It was a while before Gavrilo turned his mind to politics and political action; he was too involved with his reading of Alexandre Dumas, Victor Hugo, Sherlock Holmes. He would never lose his interest in literature, but when he was seventeen his reading tastes began to broaden. He became involved with the writings of anarchists, socialists, nihilists, and nationalists; and, as might have been expected of a young man in Sarajevo, he became politically active. He joined a Young Bosnia group and participated in antigovernment student demonstrations. He suffered a saber wound in a student battle with the Sarajevo police. Eventually, he was expelled from school.

Like so many other Young Bosnians, who found their schooling curtailed because of their antigovernment activities, the young Gavrilo Princip left Sarajevo, took to the road, and, on foot, crossed the Bosnian border and made for the Serbian capital, Belgrade.

Belgrade was a particularly exciting city when Princip got there. The students, for the most part, had no money, had little to eat, and were forced to sleep wherever they could find a place to lie down, in the parks or in the streets; but the talk at the cafes, where students gathered to drink coffee, perhaps a bit of wine when they were affluent, was animated and alive with anticipation of imminent perilous but glorious events.

The Slavs, Bulgarians, Montenegrins, and Serbians were openly preparing for a war on what was left of the Ottoman Empire in the Balkans. Serbia had ordered a mobilization of its troops. Young Slavs were crossing the borders of the Austrian territory in which they lived to volunteer for service with the Serbian army. It was a great day for the dreamers of a greater Serbia, the

Pan-Slavists, and the ultranationalists, and Gavrilo Princip was not exempt from the martial fever which swept through the ranks of Bosnian students in Belgrade.

As early as February 1912, Princip indicated a will for violent action for the liberation of the Slav people. It was at a meeting of his particular Young Bosnia group, when he was still in Sarajevo, that Princip declared he was prepared to assassinate the Austrian governor of Bosnia, General Oskar Potiorek, or the Austrian minister of finance, Leon von Bilinski. An attempt to procure the weapons for the assassination failed, however, and the political murders had to be postponed for some more propitious moment.

In October 1912, Princip, in Belgrade, attempted to enlist in the Serbian forces to fight against the Turks, but he was rejected. He traveled to Prokuplje, on the Turkish border. Here the troops under Major Vojin Tankosic were being readied for an advance onto Turkish soil. Princip offered his services, but he was turned down again.

"Too small, too weak," said the major.

Tankosic would have a more significant task for the small, weak young man, but Princip left Prokuplje deeply disappointed. He would never forget the rebuff he suffered at the hands of the major, but he would not shrink from working with him to strike a blow for the Pan-Slav cause when the time was ripe for it; and that time was not too long in coming.

At Acorn Garland, one of the Bosnian students' meeting places in Belgrade, in the spring of 1914, Gavrilo Princip sat down to lunch with his friend Nedeljko Cabrinovic. Cabrinovic gave Princip a clipping from a Sarajevo newspaper reporting the intended visit of Archduke Franz Ferdinand to the capital city of the

Bosnian province. Princip read the item but made no remark on it. Later that evening, however, sitting on a park bench with Cabrinovic, Gavrilo Princip almost casually announced that he planned to be in Sarajevo when the archduke arrived, and that he would kill him.

Perhaps less casually, he asked Cabrinovic whether he would join him in the attempt to assassinate the Hapsburg prince, and Cabrinovic, as he testified in his trial of 1914, hesitated for only a moment before he and Princip shook hands, and pledged themselves to the task.

Nedeljko Cabrinovic, a half year younger than Gavrilo Princip, was born in Sarajevo on January 20, 1895, the first of nine children born to his household. His father, a huge man and something of a brute, owned a cafe in the town. He was also—or at least the Young Bosnians believed he was—a paid informer for the Austrian police.

Even as a boy, Nedeljko ran into difficulties with his father. A fierce antagonism developed between the two with the years and certainly marked the lives of both. Savage beatings were common in the Cabrinovic house. When Nedeljko failed in his school examinations, his father beat him. When the father came upon the son reading "subversive" literature, he beat him again. Finally, when Nedeljko quit one of his numerous jobs (he had worked as a locksmith, as a lathe operator, and as a typesetter), his father beat him once more, and threw him out of his house as well.

Nedeljko was no more than fifteen years old when his father had him arrested for some breach of discipline and tossed into jail, where he was held for three days. It was obvious to Nedeljko that there could be no peace between him and his father, and after the jail episode he began to wander all over the province and beyond, picking up a job now and then at a printing shop.

He did return to Sarajevo, only to land in jail again. This time it was because he became involved in a printers' strike and was accused of plotting arson. Since he would not reveal the names of the leaders of the strike, he got himself banished from Sarajevo for five years.

For a while, before his father and the printers' union officials prevailed on the authorities to cut his banishment short, Cabrinovic worked in Belgrade. When he did return to Sarajevo, he did not stay very long: there was too much happening back in Belgrade, too much excitement and stimulation for young people. He was not slow in returning to the capital city of Serbia.

Nedeljko Cabrinovic had had little formal schooling, and some of his colleagues looked down on him with rather smug snobbery because of his lack of interest in intellectual matters. But Cabrinovic was a brilliant young man (for all his failures in school), quick and perceptive. He had not only read widely in socialist and anarchist writings; he had also published his own dissertations in political journals. Before he became a member of a Young Bosnia group, he had at different times proclaimed himself an anarchist and a socialist, and Princip, among others, was inclined to doubt the earnestness of his more recent allegiance to the Slav nationalist cause. There had been quarrels between Princip and Cabrinovic, and Cabrinovic had been ousted from a Young Bosnia club to which both young men belonged, because of political differences. The charge that Cabrinovic's father was an Austrian spy also affected what might have been a much closer relationship between the two conspirators. Nevertheless, they did agree on the assassination, and both decided that a third man was necessary for their plot. The third man was Trifko Grabez, a Young Bosnian and probably a member of the Black Hand, as most likely, too, was Gavrilo Princip (though not Nedeljko Cabrinovic, who tended to talk too much and too carelessly, and whose father, as previously noted, was suspected of being an agent for the Austrian government).

Grabez, who shared a room with Princip and other Bosnian students, was nineteen years old. He was the son of an Orthodox priest and, as he testified at his trial for his role in the Sarajevo assassinations, was educated "in the spirit of the Gospel." He would also defend the faith of his fellow conspirators at the trial, declaring that they had "a national religion of a higher type."

Trifko Grabez was another of the brilliant Bosnian students who seemed to abound in Belgrade and Sarajevo at the time. And like so many of the others, he had been expelled from school for disciplinary reasons. He had always been marked down as a rebel, and when, at the age of seventeen, he struck one of his teachers, he reaped the reward for his intemperate action. Unperturbed, Trifko Grabez departed for Belgrade to continue his studies, in which he had always done well, and to continue his rebel activities.

When Grabez was approached by Princip and Cabrinovic, there was no hesitancy in his response. He needed no persuading; he was as eager for the assassination as were his two comrades and immediately sat down with them to lay out procedures for a precise execution of the plot.

Their initial problem was that of procuring the proper arms: guns, bombs, poison. They approached Milan Ciganovic, a Bosnian who had fought with the Serbian army and had been awarded a medal for his bravery in action. He was known to have some old bombs from his fighting days stored in a box at his home.

Ciganovic was a character about whom there has been considerable speculation. He was employed in an ordinary job by the Serbian State Railways. He was a member of the fairly conservative *Narodna Odbrana* (National Defense), which had limited its activities to Slav cultural pursuits since 1909. It is not known for certain whether Ciganovic was a member of the Black Hand, but he was at least considered a trustworthy ally by the organization. Some have suggested, though, that the prime minister, Nikola Pasic, an arch foe of the Black Hand, had sent Ciganovic into the organization to spy on its secret operations. Those holding this view point out that Ciganovic acted as a government witness against Colonel Dragutin Dimitrijevic (Apis) at his trial in 1917. It is possible, however, that he was only trying to save his own life by testifying against Apis. The speculation concerning his espionage for Pasic has never gone beyond the stage of conjecture. Whatever the case, Ciganovic was to play a significant part in the assassination of Franz Ferdinand.

There is one other factor to consider in the organization of the plot to murder the archduke. It may very well be, as a number of historians have written, that the assassination was entirely conceived and engineered from beginning to end by Colonel Dimitrijevic, in order to create for Nikola Pasic a profoundly embarrassing situation and an international crisis which would topple him from power; and that the testimony of the young assassins was mostly fiction, an effort to present themselves as martyrs to their cause while protecting those in high places from retribution.

Even if the plot and its execution were completely the work of the Young Bosnians, still Apis, with his excellent and thoroughgoing espionage, would have been aware of all their activities from the very start, in which case, in his own special conspiratorial manner, he would have directed their development from behind the scene. It was unquestionably the Black Hand which provided the assassins with the murder weapons. And it seems logical that the training of Young Bosnians in the use of those weapons—learning how to shoot a revolver with accuracy, throw bombs, employ poison—took place in the Black Hand's school for partisans outside Belgrade.

In any case, according to this version, Apis, aware of the possible punitive action on the part of Austria should the archduke be assassinated, consulted with Colonel Artamonov, the Russian military attaché. What would be the position of Russia should the Hapsburgs blame Serbia for the political murder and invade its territory in retaliation? He got the answer he wanted. Artamonov assured Apis that in the event of an Austrian attack, Russia would support the Serbs.

Next, as the chief of the intelligence department of the Serbian general staff, Apis delegated a trusted lieutenant, the partisan leader Vojin Tankosic, to find among the Bosnian young men in Belgrade a team of zealots who could accomplish the projected political action. Apis wanted to keep a distance between himself and the assassins for two reasons: first, he wished to disassociate Serbia from the crime; and second, if the soldiers of the Black Hand failed, the organization itself, particularly its leadership, had to be shielded from retribution. If the first assassination attempt failed, the organization would have to be preserved, intact, in order to attempt another.

Vojin Tankosic was of the same mind. He selected the three men for the task at hand—Princip, Cabrinovic, Grabez—then handed them over to Milan Ciganovic to be trained and prepared, to be given the weapons needed for the assassination and the money with which to travel to Sarajevo to meet the archduke.

Tankosic chose carefully and well. He knew his three recruits were acquainted with each other, that they were friends. He knew that they neither drank nor gambled, that they had little, if anything, to do with women. Princip, he had been told, was actually shy in the presence of women. The partisan leader knew, too, the intensity of the Slav patriotism of the young men; he was aware of their past records, including their various scuffles with the authorities in Bosnia.

What he may not have known was that all three were suffering from tuberculosis in varying degrees of its development, and that each of the would-be assassins was aware of the disease eating away at his lungs and, in the case of Princip, his bones.

Actually, the tuberculosis was an added incentive for the young zealots. The spirit of self-sacrifice and martyrdom was very strong among the Young Bosnians. Bogdan Zerajic, the young Serb out of Hercegovina who had killed himself after his attempt on the life of the Austrian governor, General Marijan Varesanin, had been glorified in verse and story, particularly by Vladimir Gacinovic, the Serbian ultranationalist and master propagandist.

"I leave my revenge to Serbdom," were the last words spoken by Zerajic, according to the legends which grew up around his death; and the words became a slogan for the Young Bosnians. He was their first martyr, Serbia's first martyr, and they swore on his grave to avenge his martyrdom.

Gavrilo Princip had brought a handful of soil from "free Serbia" to put on his grave. All three assassination-bound Bosnians visited the grave of Zerajic before setting out on their mission.

Tuberculosis meant an early end to their lives. The three conspirators felt a burning need to contribute to their cause something of significance before that end. They dedicated the remainder of their years to what they considered a profound gesture for Serbian freedom, a martyrdom worthy of a Serbian rebel.

The Assassins Move to Sarajevo

9

DURING the month of May in 1914, Princip, Grabez, and Cabrinovic took pistol practice. Princip was particularly accurate as a marksman. He could hit his target six times out of ten at a distance of more than two hundred yards. From sixty yards he never missed. He would be considerably closer to his target on the twenty-eighth of June, 1914.

By the twenty-seventh of May, Milan Ciganovic considered his students fully educated for their mission. He gave them their weapons: four late-model Belgian revolvers, six bombs (which had come from the Serbian army arsenal at Kragujevac), and three vials of cyanide, one for each.

The bombs were of the type that could be concealed in a pocket. They were rectangular in shape, smaller than a hand gun. To set one off, the assassin would need to remove its cap, strike its detonator, wait twelve seconds, then hurl—at which moment it would explode. The cyanide was to be swallowed by the assassin to prevent his being apprehended alive by the police. Suicide was an assumed procedure on the part of the Young Bosnians, a tradition set for them by the martyr Bogdan Zerajic. Suicide was essential in the planning of Colonel Dimitrijevic and the Black Hand. There must be no investigation that would lead to the top men in the secret society; there must be no implication of the Serbian government in the assassination. Keep out of the way of any Serbian army man, stressed Ciganovic in his instructions to the three conspirators. Stay away from the Serbian police.

With Grabez, who knew the territory well, Ciganovic plotted the route which the conspirators would find safest for crossing the Serbian border and for moving on to Sarajevo; and Princip cautioned his two comrades to say nothing of their destination, and certainly nothing of their intention, even to those who were friendly along the "underground" route they were to travel. He would have to repeat that caution more than once to the restless, incautious, talkative Cabrinovic.

On May 28, each with two bombs strapped to his waist, the gun in his pockets along with the vial of cyanide, the conspirators left Belgrade and headed by a rather circuitous route to the capital city of Bosnia, and their rendezvous with Franz Ferdinand.

The first leg of their roundabout journey was by boat, along the Sava River to Sabac, a small town about forty miles west of Belgrade. It was on the boat that Princip found reason to quarrel with Cabrinovic again, and to suspect that his own decision to include Cabrinovic in the conspiracy had been an error. The sociable Nedljko, forgetting his instructions almost at once, began to talk with a Serb soldier on the riverboat, much to the irritation and perhaps fear of his comrades. Nothing came of the incident; the soldier wasn't interested in Cabrinovic's remarks and paid no attention to him. But his comrades let the talkative conspirator know how they felt about his lack of discipline.

At Sabac, they made contact with Captain Rade Popovic of the frontier guards, as Ciganovic had instructed. Popovic was an Apis man. He was shown a letter by the young conspirators, a letter bearing the initials M. C. for Milan Ciganovic, and the border guard was immediately at the service of the Bosnians. He gave them official papers which would identify them as customs officials, and a letter of introduction to Captain Jovan Prvanovic, the frontier guard at Loznica, about forty miles farther southwest, on the River Drina.

"Take care of these men and take them over wherever you think best," the letter instructed.

Why the three Bosnian youths needed to obtain these papers and the guides, and why they had to take such a circuitous route, is rather difficult to understand. As Bosnians, they were Austrian citizens and required neither passport nor visa to cross into the Austrian territory of Bosnia. For that matter, at the time, neither Austria nor Serbia required its citizens to have a passport before they could cross the border between the two countries. It would seem that the young men were caught up in the melodramatics of conspiracy. Or perhaps it was Apis who insisted on playing the game of conspiracy according to his rules or to his penchant for secrecy.

Whatever the case, the three young men spent the night in Sabac at a hotel, hiding their guns and bombs in the stove that came with their room. Again, it appears that they were acting in the spirit of the conspiratorial game, since it wasn't likely that anyone was going to search them or the room for concealed weapons.

In the morning, they retrieved their arsenal, tied the bombs to their waists, under their coats, pocketed the guns and the cyanide, and proceeded by train to Loznica and Captain Prvanovic. The captain, evidently another Apis man, considered the letter from Captain

Popovic an order. He arranged for three sergeants to report to his office in the morning and escort the three Bosnians across the border.

The conspirators had the rest of the day, and the night, too, to spend in Loznica—and to quarrel. Again, Cabrinovic was the culprit. First, they encountered a man who had fought with the partisans and who saw that Cabrinovic was carrying bombs. The man asked him where he was headed, and Princip had a hard time keeping his comrade's mouth shut. Later, when the trio took to postcard writing, both Princip and Grabez had to remind Cabrinovic of the need for caution. Princip wrote a cousin in Belgrade, saying he was going to a monastery to get himself ready for an examination. It was his way of covering his tracks, should the postcard be read by any of the authorities. Cabrinovic sent off about half a dozen postcards, at least one of which would have aroused the suspicion of the police. The conspirators quarreled and, in the morning, when the frontier sergeants suggested they split up and move in different directions, the suggestion was immediately and gladly accepted.

Princip and Grabez moved north to the border town of Ljesnica. Cabrinovic, who was relieved of his bombs by Princip, was directed to cross the border at Zvornik. Before parting, Grabez and Cabrinovic exchanged passports. Cabrinovic had been jailed twice by Austrian police and his name was familiar to them. It was thought best for the safety of the mission that Nedjelko travel with some other identification than his own should he be stopped for any reason by the authorities. Again, this gesture seems to have been part of the conspiracy play-acting. There was no need for the passports at all. And, again for no other apparent reason except to play at conspiracy, they agreed to meet in the small town of Tuzla, not in Sarajevo, their destination.

Princip and Grabez were put up for the night by the border guard sergeant in the border guard barracks at Ljesnica. On the morning of May 31, they were ferried across the River Drina to Isakovic Island. They waited at an inn on the island until three in the afternoon for their next guides, two peasants who moved them through rain-soaked, heavily wooded terrain in Indian fashion: single file and separated by twenty paces. One of the guides, Jakov Milovic, knew every step of the way. He was a smuggler and a frequent guide for the Apis underground. He could have eluded any police, if they appeared, in broad daylight—he had done it often enough; but he fell in line with the conspiratorial attitudes.

Milovic walked the two young men until they were almost exhausted. They were now on Austrian soil but still a good distance from Tuzla, where they were to meet with Cabrinovic. They slept the night in an abandoned farmhouse; then, in the rain and through the mud, they continued their journey, leaving their footprints as they went, to the outskirts of Priboj. Here they were picked up by their next guide, a schoolteacher named Veljko Cubrilovic, who was asked to provide them with a horse and a cart, for which they would pay, to transport them to Tuzla.

Cubrilovic led them to the house of a wealthy farmer, Mitar Kerovic, who was glad to oblige. His son, Nedjo, would drive the young assassins to Tuzla. Mitar knew they were assassins, and so did his son. Cubrilovic, his curiosity getting the better of his judgment, had asked directly of the two young Bosnians, "Are the bombs for the archduke?" And Princip had answered, breaching the discipline he had set for himself and his comrades,

"We are going to Sarajevo to assassinate Franz Ferdinand."

The young schoolteacher, undoubtedly proud of the role he was playing in the projected assassination, repeated the story to Mitar Kerovic and his son and showed them the bombs that were to be used. And Princip, joining the act, demonstrated to them the technique for hurling the weapon and showed them his guns as well. The Kerovics were certainly impressed, but they would pay dearly for this small moment of participation in the assassination plot.

Toward midnight, with Nedjo Kerovic at the reins, the assassins left Priboj. By early morning they were at the edge of Tuzla. Here, Princip and Grabez got off to wash in a running brook, while Nedjo went on to deposit their small arsenal with the assassins' next arranged contact. (All the contacts had been prearranged by Milan Ciganovic.) The contact in Tuzla was a very wealthy and highly respected citizen of the town, Misko Jovanovic.

Jovanovic was quite nervous, understandably, about the weapons, and promptly hid them in the attic of his house. When Princip asked him to deliver the guns and bombs to Sarajevo, he flatly refused. He did agree to hold on to them for only a few days, when they were to be picked up by a messenger bearing the proper identification, a pack of a certain brand of cigarettes.

Cabrinovic, meanwhile, had had no difficulty at all reaching Tuzla. He had met his friendly contact at Zvornik, then had simply strolled across the border into Bosnia and taken a train to the arranged meeting place. He was in Tuzla three days before his comrades arrived after their adventurous and completely unnecessary hardships.

There was a bit of a scare for Cabrinovic, however,

in Tuzla. At a cafe, the day before Princip and Grabez came into town, he had been recognized by a police officer from Sarajevo. The police officer knew him well and was well acquainted with his father. He asked Cabrinovic where he had been. Cabrinovic answered truthfully that he had been in Belgrade. Whether the officer's suspicions were aroused Cabrinovic could not say, but he reported the incident with considerable trepidation to Princip and Grabez when they arrived.

The three conspirators took the train to Sarajevo later that day, leaving their weapons in the hands of Jovanovic, to be retrieved at the appropriate time. They were in the same car but, again for security reasons, sat apart from each other. Cabrinovic's friend, the policeman from Sarajevo, was in the train, too, and made a point of sitting down next to the young conspirator, talking with him the whole length of the trip. It was only small talk, however, and Cabrinovic relaxed; so did Princip and Grabez. The officer was never aware of the mission that rode with that railroad train until after the mission was accomplished.

In Sarajevo, the conspirators separated. Grabez and Cabrinovic each went to stay with his own family. Princip went to stay with his old friend Danilo Ilic, who had already been informed by Princip, in a coded letter, of the plot to assassinate Franz Ferdinand on his arrival in Bosnia.

The date was June 3. There were twenty-five days to the ceremonial entrance of the archduke into Sarajevo and the political murders.

The Efforts to Stop
the Assassins

10

IT WAS probably early in May that Nikola Pasic, prime minister of Serbia, got word of the assassination plot, perhaps from Milan Ciganovic and certainly from Jakov Milovic, who in addition to his activities as a smuggler was a member of the *Narodna Odbrana*. Pasic acted immediately. He ordered all border guards to be on the alert for the three assassins and to stop them from crossing into Austrian territory.

The order was ignored. The guards, although they were associated with the conservative *Narodna Odbrana*, were more loyal to Apis and the Black Hand. Their reply to the prime minister's command was that it had come too late.

Pasic became increasingly disturbed by the situation; he rightly feared that the assassination of the Hapsburg archduke might very well provoke an Austrian invasion of Serbia, and that Serbia was hardly prepared for such an invasion. He called a meeting of his cabinet to deal with the situation. He ordered an investigation of the activities of Colonel Dimitrijevic (Apis). He ordered an investigation of his border guards. None of this, however, was going to stop the assassins.

The prime minister considered warning the Austrians in Vienna of the assassination plot, but this presented him with a dilemma. If he revealed the plot to the Hapsburgs, the Black Hand would learn of it soon enough, and Pasic himself would very likely become the next victim of its terror. Besides, such a revelation would serve only to increase the already strong appeal of the Black Hand among the Serbians and, at the very least, cost Pasic and his Radical Party the coming elections. There was, too, the danger of implicating the Serbian government in the plot to assassinate Franz Ferdinand, if Pasic were to send an official note to the Viennese government. The plot had originated on Serbian soil, and Serbia could be held responsible for not squelching it.

Pasic, a master diplomat, attacked his problem obliquely. He sent a message to the Serbian minister in Vienna, Jovan Jovanovic, asking him to warn the Hapsburgs of the possibility of an assassination attempt, but to make it only an informal warning, not providing any specific data.

Jovanovic was the wrong man for such a job, certainly as far as Pasic was concerned. The minister in Vienna, if not a member of the Black Hand, was very much in sympathy with the organization. He was the Black Hand candidate for the next foreign minister for Serbia. He was also very much suspected in the Austrian capital for his extremist Pan-Slavic views; the Austrians had suggested on a number of occasions that they would be pleased if Jovanovic were recalled by his government and replaced by a more amiable minister. Jovanovic did follow his instructions from Pasic, but in a manner which didn't create even a stir in Vienna.

He sought out the Hapsburg minister of finance, Leon von Bilinski, with whom he had been on fairly friendly terms. He suggested to the minister, perhaps earnestly but certainly not in official tones, that it might not be advisable for the archduke to attend the maneuvers scheduled for late June in Bosnia; that such maneuvers might be considered provocative to the Serbians, and that some misguided Serb might fire a loaded gun at "someone" he disliked. He said nothing at all of the assassins who had already crossed the Drina and who were waiting for the archduke in Sarajevo. He said nothing of the assassination plot. He had followed Pasic's orders in a way which would please the prime minister, but would please the Black Hand more.

Bilinski took his interview with Jovanovic lightly—too lightly. He didn't see how the maneuvers could possibly irritate Serbia or the Serbians, and, according to the latest information he had received, all was quiet and peaceful in Bosnia. He departed from Jovanovic in a friendly enough spirit. "Let's hope nothing happens," he said; and that was the end of it. He felt he had no reason to transmit the message he had gotten from Jovanovic, who was, in any case, suspect among the Austrians, and it died with him.

The Black Hand, too, in full executive session, made an effort to stop the Sarajevo assassination. It would seem that Apis had planned the political murders on his own, with perhaps only Major Tankosic and Milan Ciganovic aware of the plot. On June 15, with all the top members of the secret society present, Apis informed them of the assassination plot and the extent of the plan's development. Surprisingly, though, the executive committee strongly objected to the plot. Killing the heir to the Austro-Hungarian throne would surely mean war with the Hapsburgs, they argued; and, like Pasic, they knew Serbia was not prepared for such an encounter.

Apis defended his decision for the assassination vehemently, but he was outvoted. After a long and bitter debate, he accepted the majority ballot of the executive committee and agreed to recall the assassins. How earnestly he followed this agreement to stop the assassination, though, is a moot question. He did tell Major Tankosic that the political murders were to be called off, and Tankosic in turn delegated Djuro Sarac, his personal bodyguard, to inform Princip, Grabez, and Cabrinovic of the executive committee's decision. Actually, Sarac was not to deliver the message himself, but was ordered to get in touch with Danilo Ilic, who, in turn, would carry the decision of the Black Hand to the three assassins. This indirect way of doing things continued to be part and parcel of the cloak-and-dagger style of the secret organization. Eventually, all this blindman's-buff secrecy would save none of the participants in the Sarajevo killings; every one of them would be called to account for his involvement.

Danilo Ilic, too—following orders, and also perhaps for personal reasons—would make an effort to stop the assassins. He would fail, but perhaps not entirely because of any wavering of loyalty on his own part, nor of his inability to argue Princip out of his intentions. On the eve of June 28, Rade Malobabic, Colonel Dimitrijevic's top intelligence man in Austria-Hungary, visited with Danilo Ilic in his mother's home. It is certainly within the realm of possibility that Apis, on his own, had decided to ignore the majority decision of his executive board, and that Malobabic was carrying his orders to his key man in Sarajevo, Ilic.

Danilo Ilic, a few years older than Princip, was the son of a cobbler who had died when Ilic was about five years old. His mother had taken up the burden of supporting her son and herself by working at a laundry, but the boy Danilo, who was very much attached to his mother, was quick to find ways to ease her task. He worked as a newsboy, for a traveling theater, as a laborer, as a porter in different railroad stations, as a longshoreman.

He was a tall, quiet young man and a good student. He had taught school for a while, then become a newspaperman, and then a translator of literature. He was a Slav patriot, too, and had served as a male nurse in the Second Balkan War. He was an important link in the chain of Young Bosnia clubs, and was the contact for the Black Hand in Sarajevo.

On being informed by Gavrilo Princip of the assassination plot, and possibly on receiving directions from the Black Hand, Ilic recruited three more young men —Mehmed Mehmedbasic, an old hand in the game of assassination, and two students, Vaso Cubrilovic and Cvetko Popovic—as part of the political murder crew. Popovic was a brilliant eighteen-year-old high school student; Cubrilovic was a sophomore in high school and, only seventeen years old, the youngest of the assassination team. Mehmedbasic was the only Moslem in the group. He was a willing assassin, but he had already failed in one attempt at political murder. He had volunteered to assassinate the Governor of Bosnia, General Oskar Potiorek, at a meeting of Pan-Slavists in France. He carried a dagger as a murder weapon, along with a vial of poison in which he was to dip the dagger to be doubly sure in his attempt to kill the general. But as the train he was riding approached the Austrian frontier, soldiers began to search the different compartments, probably for contraband, and Mehmedbasic lost a bit of his nerve. He dumped both dagger and poison down the train's lavatory and abandoned his mission.

Danilo Ilic knew the story, but he—or the Black Hand—considered it to be good tactics to have a Moslem with the assassins. Should they be apprehended, the presence of a Moslem would show that the plot was not an all-Slav effort and that discontent with Hapsburg rule was not limited to the Slav elements, but was widespread among the inhabitants of Bosnia-Hercegovina.

Ilic, too, assumed the task of retrieving the assassins' arms from Misko Jovanovic in Tuzla. It was not a simple task, as the young teacher-newspaperman-rebel executed it; it was a rather complicated and completely roundabout process, in the typical melodramatic, conspiratorial fashion.

Jovanovic was asked to make a package of the small arsenal and to deliver it to a railroad station. Reluctantly, Jovanovic agreed, and it was decided he would meet Ilic at the Doboj station, some thirty-five miles out of Tuzla, the next morning. But Ilic was not at the appointed destination when Jovanovic got there. Nervously, Jovanovic deposited his package in the second-class waiting room of the station, his overcoat on top of it. For a while, he reconnoitered the area, then retrieved his package and left it in a tailor shop nearby. The tailor, whom he knew, was not in at the time, so Jovanovic asked an apprentice who was minding the store to keep an eye on both his coat and the package.

It was a couple of hours before the next train from Tuzla was due at the station, and Jovanovic did what he could to control his apprehensions. When the train finally did arrive, it was a very much relieved merchant who met the long-overdue Ilic, took him to the tailor shop, and got rid of the dangerous cargo he had been concealing.

Ilic continued the conspiratorial charade. With the arms for the assassination in his hands, he took the express train from Tuzla to Sarajevo, but got off the train two stops before the capital city. Here he boarded a local train which took him to the outskirts of the capital.

From there he rode a streetcar to the Sarajevo cathedral. From the cathedral he walked home, where he hid his precious package under a couch in his room. It would remain there until the night before the assassination.

Despite all this participation in the plot to murder the archduke, Ilic, for some time, had had doubts about the wisdom of it. His doubts were purely political, not humanitarian. He was not opposed to assassination as such, but he had begun to think more trenchantly of the purpose it served, or did not serve. If by assassination, he reasoned, some revolutionary good were effected, then assassination was a positive gesture. But the history of assassination, as he knew it, was the story of violence producing counterviolence, with nothing of a positive character to compensate for the bloodshed or the hardship that followed.

Ilic wavered in his thinking until the last moment. He had been encouraged by Apis—by way of Major Tankosic, by way of Djuro Sarac—to try to stop the murders, and he tried to convince both Gavrilo Princip and Trifko Grabez that their venture was not in the best interests of their cause, the freedom of the Slavs from Hapsburg rule. But, in the end, he remained loyal to his Black Hand commitments and to his responsibilities in the organizing of the assassination of Franz Ferdinand. Perhaps it was the visit of Rade Malobabic, the intelligence agent, on the eve of the assassination, which determined the final and fatal decision.

On the Eve of the Assassination

11

EXCEPT for the long discussions between Danilo Ilic and Gavrilo Princip on the philosophy of assassination as a revolutionary tactic, with Triko Grabez joining the argument now and then, the weeks waiting for the arrival of Archduke Franz Ferdinand in Sarajevo were comparatively calm. There was the moment when Princip found himself face to face with the Hapsburg, purely by accident, at the Oriental Bazaar. Princip had his gun in his pocket and might easily have shot the archduke right then and there. He didn't. He contented himself with getting a good look at Franz Ferdinand so he would not fail to recognize him at the appointed time for the assassination. Later, at his trial, he would say that he was afraid he might hit some innocent bystanders in the crowded shop. This "apology" does not hold very well, considering the kind of marksman Princip proved himself to be. More likely it was the young assassin's sense of revolutionary discipline. The assassination had been scheduled as a team effort; he was duty-bound to keep it that way. Much of the evidence given at the hearings and the trials following the political murders was meant to conceal the collaboration of accessories to the act, and, for a while, anyway, each assassin was to claim that he had acted alone, or at least independently of the others.

Cabrinovic had set out on his own to get a good look at the archduke before the assigned day for the assassination. He had traveled to Ilidze and was approaching the hotel where Franz Ferdinand and his wife were being housed, but he recognized a police agent guarding the place and thought the agent had recognized him. He spent the rest of that afternoon getting away from Ilidze and the police.

Actually, the agent had recognized Cabrinovic and reported his presence to headquarters, but headquarters was lax, as it was about all other safety precautions during the stay of the archduke. Nothing was done to keep the young Cabrinovic, known to the police for his antigovernment activities, under lock and key, or even under surveillance. And this was the case with all the other young assassins. They wandered the streets of Sarajevo unattended, unfollowed, free.

Of course, the young Bosnians did nothing to attract attention, either. They stayed in their homes reading, as Princip in particular did, or spent time at the student cafes; they met together infrequently, and then only at night.

Danilo Ilic, who had assumed the responsibility for the teamwork of the assassins—probably on orders from Apis—organized the schedule of assignments for each of his men; he would also distribute the murder weapons and the cyanide to each member of his crew.

The newspapers had printed the precise route of the royal entourage on its official visit to the city, so that the people who wanted to greet the Hapsburgs would know where to congregate. The news item made Ilic's job quite simple. The royal procession would be moving down Appel Quay, the street which led along the Miljacka River from the railroad station (where the archduke would arrive from Ilidze) to the town hall, where the grand reception had been prepared for His Royal Highness. Danilo Ilic, dividing his six conspirators into three teams of two, assigned a spot for each team, with about one hundred yards separating them. If the bombs of the first pair failed to kill the archduke, the second pair would hurl its bombs; if the first and second crew missed, it would be up to the third to accomplish the assigned mission.

Mehmed Mehmedbasic and Vaso Cubrilovic were to post themselves in front of the Mostar Cafe. Across the street, and at the prescribed distance, on the river side of Appel Quay, Nedeljko Cabrinovic was to stand with his bomb ready; opposite him, on the shore side, would be Cvetko Popovic. Gavrilo Princip's post was closer to the town hall, with Trifko Grabez nearby. The archduke's entourage was scheduled to traverse Appel Quay twice, on its procession to the town hall and on its return to the station. Should there be any difficulty meeting their assignments the first time, the assassins would be afforded a second chance.

His plans complete, Ilic waited until the Saturday, and the Sunday morning, before the scheduled royal visit to give the conspirators their final directions and their arms.

Early Saturday afternoon, he met with Princip and Mehmedbasic at a cafe and introduced the Moslem to Princip as "one of us." It was the first time Princip met any of the auxiliary assassination squad. Later that afternoon, Ilic met with Popovic and Cubrilovic, walked with them to a park at the edge of the city, gave each his gun, his bomb, and his vial of cyanide, and showed them how to use the weapons; they knew the purpose of the cyanide. Late the same evening, he gave a bomb to Mehmedbasic and again instructed him on how it worked and how he was to employ it.

It was Princip who met with Cabrinovic Saturday afternoon to give him his vial of cyanide and to instruct him on the post he was to take on Appel Quay. Because he was still in doubt of Cabrinovic's ability to keep to the necessary discipline, he stressed the importance of Cabrinovic's not moving from that post and said he would receive his bomb in the morning. For some reason, probably the discipline factor again, Cabrinovic never received a gun.

There was a party the evening of the twenty-seventh at the Semiz Cafe. Gavrilo Princip and several others of the assassination team met a group of young Bosnians, members of one of the many secret anti-Hapsburg societies in Sarajevo, to talk, sing, and perhaps drink a little wine. Princip, preoccupied with the gravity of his task in the morning, was scarcely in the mood for a celebration. But as the hours wore on, the student jibes at the Austrian authorities, the singing, the general optimism of his young Bosnian friends, reached him; and he joined in the festive atmosphere.

Toward midnight the party began to break up, but Princip was far from ready to go to bed for the night. He walked with a couple of his old comrades to their homes, embraced them, and then, suddenly realizing that it was better that they not be seen with him lest they be implicated in the assassination conspiracy, made his hasty farewells.

He was still not ready to retire for the night. He walked the long way to the Kosovo Cemetery, alone. It was in the Kosovo Cemetery that the Young Bosnians' hero, Bogdan Zerajic, "Serbia's first martyr," was buried. His grave was a shrine for Bosnia's young rebels.

At the shrine, Princip deposited some flowers which

he had managed to pick up on the way, and spent some moments meditating on the course of his life and thinking about the blow he would strike for Serbian freedom; then, in the darkness, he probably repeated his oath to avenge the "martyr's" death. He then returned home, reading for a while before retiring for the evening.

Ilic had been at the cemetery, paying his homage to Zerajic's memory, earlier in the evening. So had Nedeljko Cabrinovic.

All was ready now for the assassination in Sarajevo the morning of June 28.

The Political Murder   12

NEDELJKO CABRINOVIC was scheduled to meet Gavrilo Princip the morning of June 28 at a pastry shop they both knew. He was to pick up his bomb at eight o'clock, but he was up and out of his parents' house, where he had been staying, much earlier. He was depressed. He had had another violent quarrel with his father, this time over the issue of hoisting the flag of the Hapsburgs to demonstrate loyalty to the empire. Nedeljko was vehemently opposed to the idea, of course, and the ill-tempered words flew.

This was naturally not the mood in which the younger Cabrinovic wished to say what was likely to be his last goodby to his family. What made matters worse was that, until the flag-raising difference arose, Nedeljko had been getting along unusually well with his father. Perhaps unknowingly, he had put forth more effort than usual to create this peace. Now that the peace was broken, the unhappy Nedeljko did what he could to leave behind him some pleasant memories of his having lived in the house of his parents. Cabrinovic was undoubtedly the quickest tempered of all the conspirators; he was also the most sentimental.

He gave his watch and pocket knife to his mother, who was still angry about his fight with his father. He gave his sister Jovanka five crowns, his grandmother twenty. He explained, at his trial later, that he was very fond of his grandmother.

He told his sister that he was leaving for some distant place, and that they would never see each other again. This, too, Cabrinovic reported at his hearings. His sister had gone off alone to cry, and Cabrinovic cried, too, then left for his appointment with Princip at the cake shop. The family dog followed him, but not for long. Cabrinovic picked up the animal, returned it to the house, and closed the door on his parents for the last time.

Both Trifko Grabez and Danilo Ilic were waiting for him at the pastry shop when he got there.

Grabez asked Cabrinovic whether he knew his post. Cabrinovic knew. Later, at his hearings, he said that he had no words with Ilic.

After a few moments, Gavrilo Princip appeared and gave Cabrinovic his bomb, which Cabrinovic immediately tucked under his belt. Princip also gave him a vial of cyanide, but no gun. Nor did Cabrinovic ask for a gun.

The sentimentalist then went on another sentimental journey. He met a friend of his, Tomo Vucinovic, on Appel Quay. At Cabrinovic's suggestion, they walked to a photographer's shop, where they had their pictures taken. The pictures were ready within the hour, and Cabrinovic asked Vucinovic to give a copy to his grandmother, another to his sister, others to friends in Trieste, Belgrade, and Zagreb.

"I wanted posterity to have my picture," he later told the judge at his inquiry.

With the photographs safely deposited with his friend, Cabrinovic took his leave and walked back to Appel Quay, where—with his coat tightly buttoned to conceal his bomb—he walked up and down the street, mingling with the crowd that had come prepared to greet the Archduke Franz Ferdinand.

Trifko Grabez, who had walked with Danilo Ilic from the cake shop to the Ilic house, where he had received his gun, his bomb, and his cyanide, was already at his assigned post. Gavrilo Princip was at Appel Quay by nine in the morning. For a while he walked with Maxim Svara, an old school chum and the son of the Sarajevo attorney general; he thought walking with the attorney's son would tend to throw off any possible suspicion on the part of the police; but Svara, a good Catholic, was soon off to Sunday mass, and Princip was alone, awaiting the arrival of the archduke.

The rest of the conspirators were at their posts early, too. Their discipline, at least at the beginning of the day, was good. Taking advantage of the inadequate security measures, the conspirators were able to move in and about the crowd at will. The police either were not looking for suspicious characters or, if they were looking, didn't expect to find any; none of the conspirators was under the surveillance of the authorities during the procession of the royal cortege, either going to or coming from the city's town hall. And the conspirators were on Appel Quay for fully an hour and a quarter before Franz Ferdinand approached the area where they were awaiting him.

At about quarter past ten, and right on schedule, the six-car royal entourage neared the position on Appel Quay near the Mostar Cafe where Mehemed Mehmedbasic and Vaso Cubrilovic were posted. The conspirators, alerted by the rising cheers and shouts of the crowds in the street, readied themselves for the purpose. But neither Mehmedbasic nor Cubrilovic was able to fulfill his responsibilities, as had been arranged by the cabal. Neither threw his bomb or fired his gun.

It was the second time Mehmedbasic had failed an assigned assassination attempt. This time he explained his failure by saying that there was a police agent standing directly behind him; that if he had made the effort to hurl the bomb, the agent would have grabbed his arm and alerted the archduke's entourage, thereby preventing any further attempts by others of the assassination team.

Cubrilovic, at seventeen the youngest of the conspirators, said that he couldn't shoot his pistol, or wouldn't shoot it, for fear of hitting the duchess, the archduke's wife. Cubrilovic was a comparative innocent. He had been recruited for the backup team of assassins by Lazar Djukic, an eighteen-year-old student who was one of the top organizers of Young Bosnia secret clubs, and who had at one time been involved in an aborted plot to assassinate the Hapsburg emperor, Franz Josef. Cubrilovic's failure may have been a result of his innocence or of a failure of courage, as it was with another of the conspirators. His bomb and his gun remained in his pockets.

Nedeljko Cabrinovic did better. As the Hapsburg procession approached his position, he asked a policeman, "In which car is the archduke?" The patrolman was obliging with the information and walked on. And Cabrinovic excitedly banged his bomb against a lamppost, knocking off its detonator, and hurled it directly at the head of the Hapsburg heir. He should have waited twelve seconds before tossing the weapon, as he had been advised. He didn't. The twelve-second difference saved the archduke's life—for the moment.

Either the bomb fell behind the folded roof of the archduke's car, or the archduke deflected the bomb with his arm or his elbow. In any case, the bomb fell into the street and exploded, wounding the passengers in the car directly behind the Hapsburgs and injuring several people in the crowd as well.

Cabrinovic could not get to his gun to put the bullet in his head, again according to orders; but he managed to swallow the cyanide he was carrying, and leaped into the Miljacka River below.

Unhappily for the would-be assassin, the poison only served to make him sick, and the water in the river was low. Four men—a shopkeeper, a barber, and two policemen—jumped into the low water after him. The shopkeeper kicked him. The barber pulled a gun out of his pocket and wanted to kill him. The police, alert for once, prevented the murder and took the culprit to police headquarters, where they began to question him immediately.

They passed Gavrilo Princip on their way, and, for a quick moment, Princip thought of putting a bullet through Cabrinovic's head, and then his own, to prevent the full disclosure of the cabal and to protect his comrades. But the moment for such action passed too quickly. Cabrinovic would have to keep silent about the plot and those involved; and though he was exhausted from his efforts to assassinate the archduke, and in some pain because of his leap into the river, the unpredictable Cabrinovic did keep his silence; he told the police nothing.

On Appel Quay, after stopping to attend the wounded, the royal entourage proceeded to the town hall for the scheduled formal reception. Cvelko Popovic, who was teamed with Cabrinovic, had quickly vacated his post on hearing the bomb explode. He was ready to confess, as he did in court, later, that he had lost his nerve. He had rushed into the basement of a nearby building, deposited his bomb, and fled the scene.

Trifko Grabez and Gavrilo Princip, who might easily have thrown their bombs or fired their guns at the archduke when he left his car and walked into the street to assess the damage Cabrinovic's bomb had done, did not use any of their arsenal. Trifko Grabez may have had second thoughts about the wisdom of the assassination. He may have thought, as Danilo Ilic tried for a while to persuade him, that assassination was neither a wise nor a proper weapon for a revolutionary. At his trial, he said he did not fire his revolver because he feared throwing suspicion on people who were standing close to him in the crowded street.

Princip explained his failure to shoot by saying that, after Cabrinovic's bomb had stopped the procession, he was too far away from the archduke to get a clear shot; and that, when the motorcade resumed and passed in front of him, the archduke's car was going too fast for him to recognize the Hapsburg. Considering the dress of the archduke—his ceremonial uniform, blue tunic, high collar, and plumed hat—this explanation of Princip's is difficult to understand. Still, he was to have a second opportunity to make good the oath he had taken at the grave of the Bosnian martyr, Bogdan Zerajic.

After the bombing incident, the police made an effort to clear Appel Quay. It was one of the very few security measures taken that day to safeguard the visiting royalty, but it was far too little, and it came far too late. There were never enough police to clear the wide, cobblestoned street of the huge crowd that had gathered to shout its welcome to the Hapsburgs, nor of the conspirators who had come to kill Franz Ferdinand.

Gavrilo Princip left his assigned post and, undisturbed by the authorities, crossed the street and positioned himself in front of a delicatessen on the corner of Appel Quay and Franz Josef Street.

The royal entourage, on leaving its official reception at the town hall, was scheduled to visit the state museum. The route to the museum called for a right-hand turn off Appel Quay onto Franz Josef Street, where Princip was poised for the assassination. But the archduke had changed the plans of his hosts. He wanted to visit the aides wounded in the Cabrinovic bombing before proceeding anywhere else. This meant going to the military hospital, which necessitated a change in the route the entourage was to take. Instead of turning right at Franz Josef Street, the cars would move directly down Appel Quay, at a swift pace to make another assassination attempt much more difficult, if not impossible.

Had the chauffeur of the Hapsburg car been informed of this change in plans and route, there most likely would have been no assassination in Sarajevo the twenty-eighth of June, 1914. He was not informed.

He turned at Franz Josef Street, as he had been initially instructed. He was ordered to stop; this was not the way to the military hospital. He shifted the car into reverse and moved back slowly.

Princip, at the corner, was no more than five feet from the car, no more than five feet from his intended victim.

At first he had thought of throwing his bomb, but it was too difficult to get to, too difficult, in the crowd, to aim properly. He drew his revolver. The presence of the duchess, sitting next to the Archduke, also caused him to pause, but not for long. He fired once. He fired again.

The first shot hit the Duchess of Hohenberg in the

abdomen. The second shot pierced the jugular vein in the archduke's neck.

Princip then turned the gun on himself. He intended to kill himself, in the tradition of the "martyr" Zerajic, as well as to comply with the orders of Apis; but someone in the crowd, a man by the name of Ante Velic, grabbed Princip's right arm. A Catholic student, Danilo Pusic, grabbed him by the neck of his coat; Princip struggled free. Pusic grabbed him again, this time by the throat, and began to strangle him, but then thought better of his intentions and his passions. A crowd closed in on the assassin. Dr. Andrea von Morsey leaped out of his car in the entourage, tried to reach him, and had to use his sword to get away from the violence of what had turned into a mob scene. A police agent was hit sharply in the stomach while trying to get to Princip and needed help before he could finally apprehend him; Princip evidently had friends he did not know were in the crowd. One of them was Mihajlo Pusara, a Young Bosnian. Gavrilo Princip would try to protect him at the investigation which followed by identifying Pusara as someone he had considered a government agent.

During the turmoil which followed the shooting, Princip did manage to swallow his vial of cyanide; the poison did no more to him than it had done to Cabrinovic. Sick to his stomach and bleeding from the wounds he had received during the scuffle with the police and the spectators, Princip was finally apprehended and taken to police headquarters.

Europe Reacts: The Norm   **13**
and the Unexpected

THE POLICE quickly rounded up all but one of the assassination team, Mehmed Mehmedbasic. Mehmedbasic had managed to cross the Austrian border into Montenegro, whose people were ardently sympathetic to the Serbian cause. But Mehmedbasic talked too much, and the Montenegrin government was forced to arrest him. Its position was embarrassing. If it did not hand over the self-confessed culprit, it would be breaking the extradition treaty it had signed with Austria. If it did extradite Mehmedbasic, the Montenegrin population would be up in arms in protest. The authorities of that little country resolved the situation quite simply: Mehmed Mehmedbasic was allowed to "escape" from the prison in which he was being held, and the Montenegrin police could never find him again.

Trifko Grabez was arrested about forty miles from the Serbian border as he tried to reach Belgrade and safety. Vaso Cubrilovic was taken in a small town in western Bosnia, and Cvetko Popovic in the town of Semlin, where he had foolishly gone to hide with his parents. Princip had unthinkingly told the authorities that he lived with the widow Ilic; Danilo Ilic was arrested.

There was a host of other arrests as well. The whole

Cabrinovic family was arrested, including Nedeljko's father, the reputed informer for the Austrian police, and even his grandmother. Mihajlo Pusara was arrested. So, soon, were all the peasants and border guards who had assisted the conspirators across the Serbian border into Bosnia; and Jovan Jovanovic, the rich merchant who had stored the assassins' arms in his attic at Tuzla. There were others, leading Slav citizens in Sarajevo, almost all of them innocent. All this despite the efforts of both Cabrinovic and Princip to protect their comrades in the conspiracy, particularly the peasants who had completely unnecessarily become involved in the assassination.

The reaction of the people of Sarajevo to the political murders was, predictably, extremely violent. The mobs gathered quickly to demonstrate their grief and their anger. At first, everything was rather peaceful and in good form. They marched through the streets to the spot of the assassination, carrying black-draped Austrian flags and pictures of the archduke and the duchess and shouting their support of the empire. At the place where the murders had occurred, Appel Quay and Franz Josef Street, they listened to speeches and knelt in prayer; then they proceeded to the cathedral to kneel and pray again for the victims of the conspirators.

Once the praying was done, however, all control was gone. The mobs went on an anti-Slav rampage, beating up every Slav they met and looting and destroying any shop, cafe, or other establishment which might be owned by a Serb. Sarajevo's best hotel was almost completely destroyed. So was the Cabrinovic cafe. Even the palace of the leading Orthodox priest was heavily damaged. The police were of no help in the situation. As a matter of fact, it has been suggested that the police encouraged the rioters. It was not until General Oskar

Potiorek called three battalions and a squadron of troops into the city and declared martial law (this after some fifty people had been injured and one killed, and after tremendous property damage) that Sarajevo became its familiar quiet self again.

In Belgrade, the capital city of Serbia, the reaction to the assassinations was rather mixed—except, of course, for the hurrahs and the unconcealed joy of the Black Hand and its press. On the one hand, the Serbs, who had had no love for the archduke, were happy to hear that Franz Ferdinand had been killed; on the other hand, they feared that Austria-Hungary might hold them responsible for the murders and might launch a war against Serbia as a reprisal. Reflecting this fear, the top government officials of the country expressed the hope that it was an Austrian and not a Serbian who was responsible for the murders. To prevent any demonstrations in the streets of Belgrade celebrating the murders—demonstrations which would certainly make a bad situation worse—all theatres, cafes, and meeting halls in the city were ordered closed by ten o'clock in the evening. The government sent its message of sympathy to Vienna. Official newspapers condemned the assassins as criminals.

None of this would help to save Serbia or the Serbians from the violence they were to suffer in a very short time.

In the other capitals of Europe, the reaction to the assassination was no less apprehensive, but considerably more controlled. In Russia, Czar Nicholas II ordered a special mass to be celebrated and called for a twelve-day period of mourning for the assassinated Franz Ferdinand. Italy, which had no love for the archduke because of his anti-Italian political position, deplored the murders. King George V of England ordered mourning dress for his court for a period of a week, and there were messages of sympathy from every head of state, including Kaiser Wilhelm II of the German Empire, and the president of the United States of America, Woodrow Wilson. But notes of sympathy, special masses, and newspaper editorials did not lessen the anxiety that swept through the Continent and over to Britain with the news of the assassination in Sarajevo. There was good reason for Europe to be concerned, nervous, and fully preoccupied with the reaction of the Hapsburgs and Vienna to the events of June 28 in the small town in Bosnia.

For more than a decade Europe had been almost continously at the brink of war. The rivalries for colonies, for spheres of influence, for raw materials and foreign markets, and for naval control of the seas increasingly had the big powers at the very edge of open and bloody hostilities. The development of the Triple Alliance—Britain, France, and Russia—and the Triple Entente—Germany, Austria, and Italy—had served only to draw the battle lines, to sharpen the fear of one for the other, and to increase military preparations and the readiness to use the growing arsenals of weapons. All that was needed to set the Continent on fire, in a test of strength, was an excuse for action, a match to the fuse of the bomb on which Europe had been sitting for so long a time. The assassinations in Sarajevo might be very easily used for that excuse.

"TO HELL WITH THE SERBIANS!" This was the banner headline in one of London's leading newspapers. It depicted well enough the state of mind not only of the British people, but also of much of the population of the Continent. It was almost a cry of desperation: Keep us out of war!

But Austria-Hungary was strangely controlled. The

expected indignation of its people was comparatively mild. There were gatherings of anti-Serbian crowds, even mobs, particularly in front of the Serbian government offices, but they were easily dispersed by the police. The reaction of the court and of the emperor, Franz Josef, was almost one of indifference, far from bellicose, subdued. There would be time, given the proper diplomats and careful diplomacy, to head off a possible conflagration and keep Europe at peace.

General Oskar Potiorek had telegraphed the news of the assassination to the emperor, who was at Ischl at the time, the spa where he usually spent his summer vacations. If the emperor was surprised or shocked by the telegram, he gave no evidence of it. He simply closed his eyes for a moment and remained silent.

"Terrible!" he finally said, or at least he was reported to have said. "A higher power has restored the order which, unfortunately, I could not maintain."

The remarks attributed to the emperor are not as enigmatic as they may seem. He was undoubtedly referring to the order in which the throne of the Hapsburgs was decided. When he had married the morganatic Sophie, Franz Ferdinand had sworn an oath which prevented any of his children from assuming the throne. With Franz Ferdinand dead, the line of the Hapsburg monarchs would proceed naturally from the emperor's grandnephew, Carl. It was a problem of very little consequence, none at all as Austria's history was to develop; but for the aging and ailing Franz Josef, it was evidently a consideration of the greatest importance.

There undoubtedly were other factors affecting the old emperor's response to the assassination. He had never liked Franz Ferdinand; he had been bothered by the archduke's politics, particularly his desire to create

a tri-part empire, with the Slavs as the third autonomous state in the greater Austro-Hungarian-Slav super-
power. It is not at all unlikely that the emperor was
relieved, as were many of the archduke's numerous
enemies at home and abroad, that Franz Ferdinand
was no longer among them.

Of course there must have been the quick memory
of the many violent deaths which had come to the
Hapsburgs during his long life: the assassination of his
wife, the execution of his brother, the suicide of his only
son. Yet the old emperor never shed a tear over the
news from Sarajevo. Nor did he give any other sign or
evidence of grief, if he grieved at all for the assassination of his nephew and his nephew's wife. Strange as
this behavior on the part of the emperor may seem, the
funeral of the archduke and the duchess was stranger,
almost unbelievably bizarre.

In Sarajevo, the remains of the royal Hapsburgs were
accorded the proper ritualistic respect. Their bodies
had been embalmed by the army surgeons and placed
in metal coffins in the drawing room of the Governor's
Palace in Konak. The room was dressed in black and
appropriately draped with flowers. The proper visitors,
dignitaries of the city and of the army, came to pay
their respects.

Late in the afternoon, the bodies were blessed by the
local archbishop. Soldiers carried the coffins to their
hearses, and battalions of infantry and cavalry led the
slow and dignified procession to the railroad station,
where a special train was waiting for them.

A twenty-four-gun salute was the final military gesture of honor paid the assassinated Hapsburgs in
Sarajevo, and the train moved quickly out of Bosnia.

At Metkovic (the archduke was returning to Vienna
by the same route he had taken to Sarajevo) the coffins

were placed on a river boat and transported to the mouth of the River Narenta. Here, once again, the archduke, this time accompanied by his wife, was carried onto the battleship *Viribus Unitis* to Trieste. It was a solemn journey, and the crowds that gathered along the route of the cortege were solemn and respectful. As the battleship moved across the Adriatic, boats of all sizes and speeds moved up to the *Viribus Unitis* to pay their last respects to the assassinated royalty. In the city of Trieste, too, crowds gathered to view, with solemnity and even grief, the arrival of the royal coffins. But it was in this port city on the Adriatic, while the bodies of the archduke and the duchess were still aboard ship, that the first signs of what was to become an extraordinary procedure became evident.

Prince Alfred Montenuevo was Emperor Franz Josef's lord chamberlain. He was the man who was fully in charge of, and fully responsible for, the funeral arrangements for Franz Ferdinand and his wife. As lord chamberlain, Prince Montenuevo was in charge of much of the protocol of the court. He had been responsible for the seating of Sophie at the end of the table at court dinners, and for putting Sophie at the end of the line in the court ball processions. He was distantly related to the Duchess of Hohenberg, which peculiarly enough may have accounted for his snobbish treatment of her. Of course, the archduke had resented all the indignities heaped on Sophie, and resented Montenuevo as well. There was no love between the prince and the archduke. It would be easy enough to blame their animosity for the bizarre events which occurred in connection with the funeral ceremonies and interment of Franz Ferdinand and Sophie. It must be remembered, however, that the prince was a lord chamberlain, not the emperor of Austria-Hungary, not the uncle of the assassinated heir to the throne.

At Trieste, an order for delay came from Prince Montenuevo in Vienna. The special train carrying the bodies of the deceased was not to arrive in the capital city until ten o'clock the following evening. Evidently, Montenuevo chose this time because he knew there would be few people on the streets then, which would make any kind of official pomp rather difficult.

Prince Montenuevo also planned to have Franz Ferdinand's body placed in Capuchin Crypt—where most Hapsburgs of recent times had been entombed—but not Sophie's. Sophie was not a Hapsburg; accordingly, claimed Montenuevo, she could not lie with her husband.

But the prince failed in this last indignity to the archduke's duchess. Franz Ferdinand had had a crypt built some seventy miles from Vienna, at his castle in Artstetten. He had specifically requested in his will that he and Sophie be laid side by side in that crypt on their deaths.

Montenuevo could not fight the will. Nor could he stop a joint requiem mass for the archduke and his wife, though he tried. He did, however, manage to carry through a number of other petty decisions, all meant to cut down on the honors normally given on such an occasion and particularly to minimize the honors for the duchess.

The coffins, he ordered, were to be brought to the designated chapel after dark. There were to be no special ceremonies at the railroad station or en route. There were to be as few soldiers as possible stationed on the streets to be traveled by the cortege. The Hofburg chapel, where the royal pair were to lie, would be open for one day only, and for only four hours, from eight in the morning until noon. Perhaps the most unwarranted of Prince Montenuevo's humiliating gestures was the manner in which the bodies of the archduke and Sophie were placed in the royal chapel. They were put side by side, probably by some oversight, but the coffin of the duchess was positioned at a lower level than that of her husband. Montenuevo had placed on the coffin of the archduke the crown of an imperial prince, a general's cap, and the archduke's hat, sabre, and medals. On the coffin of the duchess he had simply placed her white gloves, her fan, and the medals and regalia, not of the wife of the heir apparent to the throne of Austria-Hungary, but of a mere lady in waiting. And Montenuevo did not give the people of Vienna even the meager four hours he had assigned for the viewing of the royal catafalques; he closed the door of the church at ten o'clock, leaving a disappointed and angry crowd in the streets.

There was more. Using as an apology the need to spare the old emperor the stress and strain of elaborate ceremonies, he informed the foreign embassies in Vienna that Franz Josef would prefer to have a simple requiem celebrated at the chapel, and that no foreign royalty or their representative missions were to be asked to attend.

By fifteen minutes past four that afternoon, the requiem was done, and the old emperor was the first to leave the chapel. The doors of the church were closed against any other callers, and the bodies were to be removed for their Artstetten destination, again by Montenuevo's orders, at the late hour of ten in the evening.

But Montenuevo did not have it all his own way. Despite the many enmities the archduke had developed in the capital, despite the general lack of love for Franz Ferdinand and Sophie in the court of Vienna, it was a Hapsburg and his wife who had been murdered, and the sentiment of the people of the capital city, its army, and its notables could not be held completely in check by the rather pernicious Prince Alfred Montenuevo.

Archduke Carl, Franz Ferdinand's nephew and the new heir to the throne of the empire, waited at the railroad station for the arrival of his assassinated uncle and aunt. So did all the off-duty officers of the Vienna garrison. They turned what might have been a very dreary and scarcely noticed cortege into a brilliant procession as the hearses moved from the railroad station to the Hofburg chapel. Lancers, royal guards with drawn swords, courtiers in carriages and on horseback accompanied the coffins to the chapel. It was the kind of reception neither the archduke nor Sophie had ever received while they were alive.

There was a similar demonstration of respect, if not sympathy, for the assassinated royal couple when their coffins were moved out of the chapel and transported to the train which was to carry their remains to Artstetten. Montenuevo had decreed that there be no military honors in the procession, because both coffins were traveling in the one cortege; by protocol, the presence of Sophie's corpse prohibited such honors. However, the lord chamberlain conceded a point to the army, probably because of his experience with his initial ban. If their officers wished, he said, the troops of the Vienna garrison might line the streets leading to the railroad station. The officers wished it, and the route to the station became brilliant with the dress uniforms of the Austrian soldiers. And, for all the efforts to the contrary by Prince Montenuevo, hundreds of men and women of the noblest families in the history of the empire joined the cortege. The populace which came out to bid farewell to the archduke and his wife was equally impressive, silent and respectful as always in the face of grief.

Montenuevo was now done with whatever ceremonies he needed to endure in Vienna. The funeral cortege, however, was still to suffer a near disaster because of the lord chamberlain's disrespectful arrangements.

The train carrying the coffins arrived in Pöchlarn at two o'clock in the morning. Pöchlarn was as near to Artstetten as the railroad trains traveled. Here, despite the hour and the darkness, a huge gathering of citizens awaited the return of the archduke and his wife to the archduke's favorite castle. They had scheduled a brief religious service to be held outdoors as the coffins were removed from the train, but a sudden, violent thunderstorm and a torrential rain cancelled their plans. Instead, the ceremony was performed in the railroad station's waiting room with most of those who had come to honor the deceased remaining in the soaking rain and the violent storm.

The rituals in the waiting room over, eight black horses pulled the royal hearse over hills, through mud, the storm still raging, to the Pöchlarn ferry, the assembled citizens following with considerable difficulty. The ferry journey, in the blackness of the night, punctuated by bolts of fierce lightning and the crashing of thunder, was to provide the last indignity to the embalmed bodies of the archduke and the duchess.

The horses hitched to the hearse were nervous and jittery, and they needed constant calming as the small boat made its slow way across the water. Nevertheless, they were fairly well controlled until the ferry reached the halfway point in the river. It was here, right in the middle of the Danube, that a particularly vicious bolt of lightning, followed by an even more vicious crash of thunder, panicked the horses momentarily and sent their precious cargo, the royal hearse, tipping toward the river. Only the alertness of some passengers, loyal followers of the archduke and his wife, kept the carriage—and the royal caskets—from going overboard.

The frightened animals were quieted and the hearse righted, and the ferry finally made a safe landing on the Artstetten side of the river. By late morning, the storm gave way to the sun, and all went well for the final interment and for the mourners who had traveled from Vienna to assist in the final rites. The soldiers who carried the coffins into the crypt did manage carelessly to crack an edge of the vault, a small piece of stone, but it was not a serious incident, and the Archduke Franz Ferdinand and his wife Sophie, Duchess of Hohenberg, were laid to rest together.

There were some rumblings of criticism in Vienna as to the manner in which Prince Alfred Montenuevo had handled the funeral proceedings for the royal couple, but the Emperor Franz Josef was quick to still it.

"For a number of years now," he wrote the lord chamberlain, "you have headed my court administration in the full possession of my confidence. . . .

". . . the passing away of my beloved nephew, Archduke Franz Ferdinand . . . has given you one more opportunity to prove your great and unselfish devotion to my person and my house.

"I am glad to have this occasion to assure you of my most cordial gratitude and of my full appreciation of your excellent and faithful service."

The letter was written on July 6, 1914. It was not until July 9, three days later, that Vienna would finally send a minor official from its foreign office to Sarajevo to make an official investigation of the assassination.

Investigation   14

THE INVESTIGATION of the plot to assassinate the archduke of Austria was begun even before the bullet of
Gavrilo Princip severed the Hapsburg's jugular vein.
Immediately after Nedeljko Cabrinovic's bomb missed
its mark, the young conspirator was grabbed by the
police, saved from a mob lynching, and dragged to police headquarters. Here his interrogation by Judge Leo
Pfeffer began at once.

Cabrinovic, in true conspiratorial style, asserted that
he was operating alone, that he had no accomplices,
that there had been no plot. But only a few minutes
later, Princip, torn and bleeding, was brought into police headquarters. Judge Pfeffer's job had broadened,
but it had not been simplified. Princip, too, claimed he
was operating on his own, that he had planned the
assassination of the archduke alone, and that he had had
no accomplices. When the judge asked about the bomb
throwing which had preceded his shooting, Princip denied any connection with the perpetrator, saying only:
"He must have felt the way I did about the Hapsburgs."

The first questions had been put to the conspirators
before either they or the judge was informed of the
death of the archduke and Sophie. When they were
told of the success of the assassination plot, Cabrinovic

gave evidence of neither satisfaction nor regret. "I aimed specifically at the archduke," he said, "in order to kill him . . . an enemy of the Slavs . . . especially of the Serbs."

Princip acknowledged his guilt in the slayings, but expressed regret for the death of the duchess.

"I am sorry that I killed the duchess of Hohenberg. I had no intention of killing her."

The questioning continued all afternoon and into the evening.

Cabrinovic finally admitted that he had known Gavrilo Princip for three or four years, that they had talked often; but he insisted that they had never spoken of terror as a political weapon, and certainly never of assassination. If Princip had been plotting to kill the archduke, Cabrinovic said, he had never discussed his intentions.

When Cabrinovic was pressed for information on where he had obtained his bomb, the conspirator was utterly vague. He said that some anarchist in Belgrade had given it to him. No, he did not know the anarchist's name.

The prisoners were removed from police headquarters and transferred to the prison of the military camp on the outskirts of the city, where they were put in chains. The interrogation continued.

On Monday, June 29, the investigation broadened. Cabrinovic finally admitted he had conspired with Gavrilo Princip to commit the political murder in Belgrade. Princip slipped in his testimony and informed the authorities that he lived with the widow Ilic; the slip brought the quick arrest of his "best friend," Danilo Ilic.

Later that day, Princip was told that Cabrinovic had admitted to their collusion in the plot, and that he had named the man who had supplied them with the arms for the assassination, Milan Ciganovic. Princip quickly changed his testimony and confessed to his association with Cabrinovic. Perhaps he thought the investigation would be closed by his confession, thereby ending the pursuit of the rest of his comrades and saving his good friend Danilo Ilic.

He was wrong. Within two days of the assassination, Judge Pfeffer had learned the names of the other conspirators. Ilic was picked up by the police on Wednesday, July 1. Trifko Grabez, admitting his guilt in the plot, was arrested the same day. Four days later, Vaso Cubrilovic was apprehended, and, on June 5, Cvetko Popovic. Mehmed Mehmedbasic was the one conspirator that could not be reached.

In prison, the conspirators managed to keep their inquisitors a bit off-course. By communicating with each other, using a code of signals they apparently all knew (an alphabetical system of wall-taps), they kept to a single story. However, as the circle of arrests broadened to include the relatively innocent peasants who had helped the conspirators cross the Austrian border, as well as people who were completely innocent of implication in the assassination, Gavrilo Princip decided to tell the authorities "the whole truth."

But the "whole truth," as Princip delivered it, was far from the truth he might have told. He named the men of the assassin team, those recruited in Belgrade, and those recruited by Ilic in Sarajevo. He did not give the names of, nor even mention, the border guards, the peasants, or the businessman of Tuzla, Jovan Jovanovic.

It was Ilic who, losing his poise rather quickly, had originally given the names of all the conspirators to Judge Pfeffer. It was Ilic, too, who mentioned in an unguarded moment the name of the man who had hidden the assassins' weapons in Tuzla. When Jovanovic was brought to Sarajevo and, without too much pressure, admitted his role in the assassination, the whole skein of the plot began to unravel almost completely, and the military jail began to fill to capacity.

There were, however, two names which notably escaped mention at the time. One was Major Vojin Tankosic, the man who was responsible for arming and training the assassins. Eventually, though, even Tankosic was identified and arrested. But not once did any of the conspirators offer the name of Colonel Dragutin Dimitrijevic (Apis) or speak of the secret terrorist organization, the Black Hand.

The investigation by Judge Leo Pfeffer had come to an end, with no evidence at all of possible Serbian government implication in the murders. It was evidence of Serbian responsibility which the Austrians had been most eager to find.

General Oskar Potiorek had kept Vienna informed of the investigation into the assassination, sending summations of the proceedings as often as twice a day, but there was nothing in his reports which would reasonably permit the capital to take the action it desired: an ultimatum to Belgrade, demanding that Serbia put a stop to its anti-Austrian activities, open and secret. There was sufficient evidence to fix the suspicion that such Serbian activities were in part, if not entirely, the inspiration for the assassination: but Vienna could offer the world no concrete proof of Serbia's guilt.

On June 10, almost two full weeks after the assassination, the Austrians finally sent a career officer in its foreign ministry, Friedrich von Wiesner, to investigate the proceedings.

Von Wiesner was a diligent worker. For two days and nights he labored through the countless pages provided him by Judge Pfeffer. He slept hardly at all. But, for all his toil, he produced practically nothing, certainly nothing which called for the drastic action the Austro-Hungarian Empire was soon to take.

The conscientious career man for all purposes simply summed up the findings of Judge Pfeffer's interrogation. With the aid of Milan Ciganovic and Vojin Tankosic, the assassins had prepared themselves for the political murder, the murder having been plotted in Belgrade. He named the border guards, peasants, and others who had assisted the conspirators in one way or another, and how they had aided them. But, he added (significantly, and to the disappointment of the strong anti-Serbian movement in Vienna):

"There is nothing to indicate, or even to give rise to the suspicion, that the Serbian government knew about the plot, its preparation, or the procurement of arms. On the contrary, there are indications that this is impossible."

Nikola Pasic, the prime minister of Serbia, who had been watching the proceedings from Belgrade with considerable anxiety, breathed a long sigh of relief on hearing of von Wiesner's report to Vienna. The threat of an immediate and profound crisis with which Serbia would need to deal, should the Hapsburgs decide on an ultimatum, seemed to have passed.

The sigh of the prime minister was premature. The great crisis Belgrade would have to meet was still in the making.

Ultimatum   15

FOR A short while, a very short while, the Hapsburgs considered their relationship with the Serbians good, or at least tolerable. In 1881, thanks to Prince Milam, the chief of state of Serbia, and his secret treaty with Vienna, Serbia was virtually a vassal state of the Austro-Hungarian Empire. In 1885, when Milam foolishly attacked Bulgaria and was soundly beaten for his folly, the Austrians intervened and prevented the Bulgarians from overrunning the Hapsburg protégé. Thereafter, the relationship between Austria-Hungary and Serbia deteriorated, eventually developing into a mutual distrust that at times gave way to overt hostility. With the rise of Serbian nationalism, the Greater Serbia movement, and the Pan-Slav movement, the Hapsburgs began to see Serbia, with its large holdings of Slav-populated territories, as a threat to the Empire.

As early as 1901, the militant Austro-Hungarian Field Marshal Conrad von Hötzendorf met with his German counterpart, General Helmuth von Moltke, to suggest that the two countries plan joint war action against Serbia and Serbia's unofficial protector, Russia.

In 1908, von Hötzendorf welcomed the Belgrade street demonstrations which protested the Hapsburg annexation of Bosnia and Hercegovina and which called for war against Austria-Hungary. Pointing to the demonstrations as evidence of the Serbs' potential threat to the empire, he proposed that Serbia be liquidated and divided between Austria and its ally, Bulgaria. Calmer heads prevailed, however. Count Stephen Tisza, the Hungarian prime minister, who almost consistently opposed the addition of any more Slav territory or Slav people to the empire, argued that an invasion of Serbia would involve Austria-Hungary in a war with Russia, a war the Hapsburgs did not relish; and the belligerent field marshal was contained for the moment.

In 1912, the Austrians, worried by Serbia's open intention of going to war with Turkey, sent a note urging the Serbians to keep the peace. The note carried a concealed threat of intervention. The Hapsburgs were not happy with the developing Serbian military strength. They certainly did not wish to sit by and watch that strength grow or the size of Serbian territory increase by way of conquest. Russia had joined with Austria-Hungary in the message to Belgrade, but the message came too late. The conflict between the Serbs and the Turks had already begun in the first of the Balkan wars of 1912–13. However, the Hapsburgs did intervene eventually in order to keep down Serbia's demands on the defeated Ottoman Empire and to minimize Serbian aggrandizement of Ottoman territory.

By the winter of 1913 and the spring of 1914, with Serbia flexing its muscles following its victory over Bulgaria in the second of the Balkan wars, and with General Conrad von Hötzendorf pressing more than ever for an invasion as a solution to the irritating and dangerous Serbian problem, the continent of Europe became alive with a quickening intrigue and the readying for military action. The long-expected great European war was at hand, and every capital on the Continent—and London, too—was aware of it.

Austria-Hungary set about seriously strengthening Bulgaria as a possible second front against the Serbians. This was not to the liking of Rumania, which was at odds with the Bulgarians, but the Hapsburg foreign office relied on the secret treaty binding the Rumanians to the empire to quiet their protests.

Kaiser Wilhelm II of the German Empire suggested that the Austrians bribe Serbia with promises of trade advantages to mute the Serbian belligerence, but he did nothing to slacken the speed with which Europe approached the great war.

On February 14, 1914, Gottlieb von Jagow, secretary of state at the foreign ministry in Berlin, wrote to Prince Karl Max Lichnowsky, Germany's ambassador in London, "We have not built our fleet in vain. . . . England will seriously ask whether it will be without danger to play France's guardian angel against us."

Germany was already prepared to attack the French, but Britain was not asleep. Lord Richard Haldane had created an Expeditionary Force of one hundred fifty thousand men, prepared to move to France on signal should it become necessary.

"If Germany attacks France, Britain will go to its aid," Prince Lichnowsky reported to his home office.

Early in June 1914, Czar Nicholas II made a state visit to Rumania, undoubtedly to weaken the link between the Rumanians and the Triple Alliance of Germany, Austria-Hungary, and Italy. The meetings between the czar and King Carl of Rumania were viewed with considerable suspicion by Theobald von Bethmann-Hollweg, the German chancellor.

After the assassination of Franz Ferdinand and his

wife in Sarajevo, although there was still no visible increase in military activity, the tempo of the intrigue
and diplomatic action picked up considerably.

The immediate response of Wilhelm II to the political murders was an angry, "Now or never! The Serbs
must be disposed of, and right soon!" He had been one
of the few friends of the assassinated archduke, and he
was unquestionably upset by his violent death. He
would approach the situation more calmly and in a
more deadly fashion after a short while, but he was at
the moment sufficiently enraged to send off a message
full of fury to Vienna.

Germany, he wired, was prepared to go to war with
France and Russia if "complications" followed an Austrian declaration of war against Serbia.

That declaration would be a while in coming.

On the twenty-ninth of June, one day after the assassination, von Hötzendorf and the Austro-Hungarian
foreign minister, Count Leopold Berchtold, agreed
that the time to crush Serbia was "now." But the Hungarian prime minister, Count Stephen Tisza, was not so
certain. He wanted guarantees of support from both
Bulgaria and Rumania before risking a possible war
with the Russians.

Count Leopold Berchtold approached the Germans,
hoping their support would satisfy the doubts of Tisza
and win his approval for an attack on Serbia. Berchtold
got better than he expected.

The kaiser had been getting notes from his ambassador in Vienna, who had been urging caution and mod-
eration.

"Tschirschky [Heinrich von Tschirschky] will be so
good as to drop this nonsense," was the kaiser's response. "We must finish with the Serbs quickly," he
repeated.

On July 5, he received two notes from Austro-Hungarians. One, from Tisza, suggested enlisting Bulgaria into the Triple Alliance. The second, from Emperor Franz Josef, proposed the crushing of Serbia.

The kaiser's response all but ignored Tisza's note. He was more interested in the effect an Austro-Hungarian march on Serbia would have on the broader European picture.

"The attitude of Russia would be hostile in every respect," he said, but that had been expected for years. "Even if war should occur between Austria-Hungary and Russia, Austria might be assured that Germany would side with her." If the Hapsburgs should decide to march against Serbia, he added, its armies would march at once.

The kaiser had given the Austrians what came to be called the "blank check." He had made it plain that he would support the Hapsburgs in any military action, even if it called for a general European war.

Still, Austria-Hungary did not act.

On July 13, von Wiesner reported to Vienna on his investigation of the assassinations in Sarajevo. Despite his findings that the Serbian government was not involved in the murders, Berchtold and von Hötzendorf would not be swayed from their decision to invade Serbia. They were finally able to convince Tisza, with the aid of the German "blank check," that the empire had nothing to fear from their projected adventure. On July 14, the German ambassador in Vienna reported to Berlin that the Austrians were preparing an ultimatum to be delivered to Serbia—an ultimatum "which would almost certainly be rejected"—and that war was imminent.

The Russian ambassador in Vienna got word of the ultimatum in preparation and warned his German counterpart that Austria-Hungary ought not to forget that if it "was absolutely determined to disturb the peace" it would "have to reckon with Europe." "Russia," said Sergei Sazonov, the Russian ambassador, "could not look on indifferently at any move which aimed at the humiliation of Serbia."

This was July 21, 1914. The same day, Raymond Poincaré, president of France, who was visiting in the Russian capital, St. Petersburg, spoke gently but firmly with the Austrian ambassador in Russia.

"With a little good will, this Serbian business is easy to settle. But it can just as easily become acute. Serbia has some very warm friends in the Russian people. And Russia has an ally, France."

Despite the words of caution on the part of the Russians and the French, despite the still far from decided knowledge of what the British would do in the event of war, despite the von Wiesner report exonerating the Serbian government, there was no stopping the machinations of Berchtold and von Hötzendorf, the Austrian hawks.

At 6:00 P.M., July 23, 1914—almost a full month after the assassinations in Sarajevo—Vienna delivered its ultimatum to Belgrade. Its terms were such that even Count Alexander von Hoyos, Berchtold's chief advisor, was forced to admit that "no nation that still possessed self-respect and dignity could possibly accept them."

This was no accident. The ultimatum was prepared under the careful guidance and scrutiny of the war-hungry foreign minister of Austria-Hungary and the commander in chief of its armies.

Following a preamble of charges, which for all purposes held the Serbian government accountable for the Sarajevo assassinations, the Austro-Hungarians listed ten points on which it demanded immediate Serbian compliance:

1. The Serbian government must suppress all publications inciting hatred of Austria-Hungary and directed against her territorial integrity.

2. The Serbian government must forthwith dissolve the *Narodna Odbrana* (the cultural society, National Defense) and confiscate all its means of propaganda against Austria-Hungary, and prevent its revival in some other form.

3. The Serbian government must eliminate from its educational system anything which might foment such propaganda.

4. The Serbian government must dismiss all officers or officials guilty of such propaganda, whose names might be subsequently communicated by Vienna.

5. The Serbian government must accept the collaboration, in Serbia, of Austro-Hungarian officials in suppressing the subversive movement against the monarchy's territorial integrity.

6. The Serbian government must open a judicial inquiry against those implicated in the murder of the archduke Franz Ferdinand and the Duchess of Hohenberg and allow delegates of Austria-Hungary to take part in the inquiry.

7. The Serbian government must immediately arrest Major Tankosic and Milan Ciganovic, implicated by the Sarajevo inquiry.

8. The Serbian government must put an effectual stop to Serbian frontier officials' sharing in the illicit traffic in arms and explosives, and dismiss the officials who had helped the assassins in their passage at Sabac and Loznica.

9. The Serbian government must explain the "unjustifiable" language used by high government officials after the murder.

10. The Serbian government must notify Vienna of the execution of all these demands without delay.

There was no mention of Colonel Dragutin Dimitrijevic (Apis), chief of the intelligence department of the Serbian general staff. Neither was there any mention of the secret terrorist organization, the Black Hand. The conspirators had succeeded in concealing the involvement of both the society and its leadership from the Austrian police and from the official investigations into the assassinations in Sarajevo.

At this time—late July, 1914—Serbia was in the midst of an election campaign. Nikola Pasic, perhaps purposely absenting himself from the capital—to avoid contact with Hapsburg officials or any direct communication with Vienna—was away from Belgrade on a campaign tour. So were most of the members of his government's cabinet. Baron Vladimir von Giesl, Austria's minister to Serbia, found himself knocking at the doors of empty offices in his quest to deliver Vienna's ultimatum. Finally, after considerable traveling, he discovered the minister of finance, Pacu, at his desk, and made his formal presentation.

Pacu, however, was not very cooperative in receiving the state message from the Austrian. He suggested that he was not the proper person, that he did not have the authority to accept such an important document. He tried, as best he could, to delay the inevitable. All the ministers were out of the capital, he made an effort to explain, all over the country, making campaign speeches for the coming election. It would take some time to recall them all to Belgrade.

Pacu, the finance minister, made a brave attempt. It did not work.

"If you won't take it," said the impatient Austrian baron, indicating the ultimatum, "I'll leave it."

And he did just that. He deposited the ultimatum on Pacu's desk and departed.

When the minister of finance and the two other members of the cabinet who had suddenly materialized read the Austrian document, they realized that there was no time at all to be lost in getting Pasic back to Belgrade. The ultimatum in their hands gave the Serbians just forty-eight hours, until 6:00 PM on July 25, to respond to the demands of the Austro-Hungarian Empire.

The tragedy in Sarajevo was giving way quickly to the most critical moment Europe had faced since the days of Napoleon Bonaparte.

Mobilization

16

NIKOLA PASIC, Serbia's prime minister, was perhaps surprised to discover that the Austrians had not mentioned the Black Hand in their ultimatum, that they had not demanded its suppression or called for the arrest of its leader, Colonel Dragutin Dimitrijevic. Pasic must have found it rather difficult to understand how the Hapsburg intelligence corps could have failed to unearth the connection between a leading personality in the Serbian army's general staff, other leaders in Serbia's governmental offices, and the assassinations in Sarajevo. Still, this failure on the part of Austrian intelligence offered Serbia a bit of breathing space in its negotiations with the Hapsburgs, and Pasic was grateful for it. Certainly, he knew, the fact that the ultimatum did not mention the Black Hand and its top echelon prevented a worldwide condemnation of Serbia as the perpetrator of the June 28 political murders. On the contrary, it allowed for a general sympathy on the Continent for the Belgrade government in the face of the harsh demands of the Austro-Hungarian Empire. It was, to all appearances, the case of a big power bullying a small and comparatively defenseless little nation of Slavs.

In Rome, the Italians—tied to Austria and Germany

in their Triple Alliance—immediately announced that they would not be obliged to take part in any war which might result from the Hapsburg ultimatum to Belgrade. Their membership in the Triple Alliance, the Italians said, required them to provide military assistance only in the event of an act of aggression against Austria or Germany.

The French, with their eyes on Germany and not without their own desires for a war that might enable them to regain the provinces of Alsace and Lorraine, which they had lost to the Prussians in the War of 1870–71, were milder in their response to the news of the Austrian ultimatum to Serbia. It expressed sympathy for the Hapsburg position and simply sent a message over the wires to Belgrade suggesting that the Serbians ask for an extension of the time limit the Austrians had set for the Serbs.

The British responded with suggestions for diplomatic action to prevent, it hoped, the development of a general European war. Sir Edward Grey, the British secretary of foreign affairs, who was already involved with a critical situation in Ireland, announced, first, that England could not take any direct action in the Balkan crisis. He announced, too, that Britain would not support a war on behalf of Serbia. This statement was made, undoubtedly, for the benefit of both Russia and France, who were pressing for a military commitment from Britain in the event of a European conflict. More positively, however, Grey proposed that the Big Four powers—Britain, France, Germany and Italy—mediate the problem.

Actually, Grey was profoundly shocked by the terms of the Austrian ultimatum. "Any nation that accepted conditions like that," he said to Prince Lichnowsky, the German ambassador to London, "would cease to count as an independent nation." He indicated to the ambassador that Britain might well accept a localized war between Austria and Serbia, but that military action involving Austria and Russia would mean a full European conflagration.

Germany's reaction to Britain's request for four-power mediation of the problem was not very reassuring. If there were difficulties between Austria and Russia, Berlin replied to the British, mediation would be appropriate and in order, since Russia and Austria were of equal stature in the family of nations. But Austria and Serbia, Berlin stressed, were not equals, and mediation of a difference between unequals would be entirely inappropriate.

The German reaction was exactly what might have been expected in London. After all, Berlin had handed Vienna a "blank check"; whatever action the Hapsburgs took, they were assured of German support. The German general staff had been preparing for war for a long time. Not only were they ready for it, they were eager for it.

In Russia, the reaction to the Vienna ultimatum to Serbia was unmistakably angry. The Russian foreign minister, Sergei Sazonov, was in a fury. "This means a European war!" he shouted. In language which was hardly temperate or diplomatic, he charged Austria-Hungary with "criminal bellicosity." The French ambassador in St. Petersburg, Maurice Paléologue, seeing in a general European war the possibility of the long hoped for "revenge" of France's defeat at the hands of Germany in 1870, did nothing to defuse the fury of the Russian minister. On the contrary, he urged him on, and Sazonov obliged.

In a face-to-face meeting with the German ambassador to Russia, Count Friedrich von Pourtales, Sazonov accused the Austrians of planning to eat up the Balkans, and Germany of conniving in the plot. As a matter of fact, he suspected that Germany, on her own, was interested in making a meal of the Balkan territories.

The evening of the day on which he had damned Austria to the German ambassador, Sazonov met with Serbia's minister to Russia, Spalajkovic, and informed him that Serbia could expect full Russian support in whatever action it took. He also urged Spalajkovic to inform Belgrade that Russia favored the rejection of the demands in the Austro-Hungarian ultimatum.

Sazonov took one more measure of significance on that busy and furious day, July 24, 1914: he proposed an immediate mobilization of the Russian armed forces, just one small step from an outright declaration of war.

On the twenty-fifth of July, the Russian council of ministers met to consider Sazonov's proposal. A bit more controlled than the foreign minister, they nevertheless agreed on an alert, a measure preliminary to total mobilization. In the event of an attack by Austria against Serbia, however, they approved of an immediate mobilization of troops on the Austro-Hungarian borders. For the time being, there was to be no belligerent gesture directed at the German Empire.

In Belgrade, meanwhile, there had been almost utter confusion. The immediate reaction to the Austrian ultimatum was one of almost complete despair. There was nothing they could do, the Serbs felt, but die fighting.

There were second thoughts, however. Fighting against the Austro-Hungarian Empire was a futile and utterly senseless project; it could accomplish nothing but a thorough defeat at a horrible cost to the Serbian people. Despite assurances from Russia, there was considerable sentiment for accepting the demands of

Vienna, with reservations if possible, unconditionally if necessary. The news of Russian mobilization plans stiffened the spines of the Serbs a bit; they ordered a mobilization of their own troops as a precaution against an abrupt Austrian attack, and at 5:58 PM, July 25, 1914, exactly two minutes before the expiration of the time allotted to Belgrade, the Serbians handed Austrian ambassador, Baron Giesl, their response to the Hapsburg ultimatum.

It was a conciliatory response, as had been urged on the Serbian government. Five of the Hapsburg demands were accepted without reservation. Belgrade accepted four of the other demands with a request for clarification. The sixth demand, which permitted Austro-Hungarian delegates to participate in a judicial inquiry into the assassinations at Sarajevo, was rejected. However, Belgrade stressed, it was willing and ready, "as always, to accept a peaceful agreement by referring this question either to the decision of the International Tribunal at the Hague (in Switzerland), or to the great powers which took part in drawing up the declaration made by the Serbian government on March 31, 1909." March 31, 1909, was the date on which Serbia formally agreed to relinquish its opposition to Austria-Hungary's annexation of Bosnia-Hercegovina.

Among the demands Belgrade asked to be negotiated was the request for the arrest of Milan Ciganovic. Major Vojin Tankosic had been apprehended, but Milan Ciganovic was nowhere on the scene; nor was he ever to be found, by Serbia, by Austria-Hungary, or by anyone else; he simply disappeared (under his own name, anyway) from history.

The demand Serbia rejected completely, if met, would have meant the end of the independence of the Serbs and would have given over the country to the

Hapsburg military, and Hapsburg domination. It was a demand Austria-Hungary knew Serbia would have to deny.

Baron Giesl, receiving the Belgrade reply to the ultimatum, scarcely looked at it. He knew that Serbia could not possibly accept its provisions in full, as the Hapsburgs had demanded. He had already prepared the note he was to give the Serbian government, a note breaking off relations between Austria-Hungary and Serbia (again a step short of outright war). His bags were packed.

Baron Giesl glanced at Belgrade's response to Vienna; handed in his note severing diplomatic relations between the two capitals; saw to it that his secret code books were burned to ashes; then left to catch the 6:30 P.M. train out of the Serbian capital.

It took the express no more than ten minutes to cross the Danube into Austro-Hungarian territory, and, at 6:45 P.M., just forty-seven minutes after receiving Belgrade's answer to the Hapsburg ultimatum, he was on the phone, talking with Count Stephen Tisza, prime minister of Hungary, informing him of what had just taken place.

Tisza was not particularly happy with what he heard. He was still hoping that some peaceful settlement of the conflict could be reached. Even Count Leopold Berchtold, the Austrian foreign minister, might have been happier with a peaceful solution to the problem. But the militant Baron Franz Conrad von Hötzendorf, field marshal of all Austria-Hungary's military might, was delighted with the word from Baron Giesl. He ordered an immediate mobilization of his troops on the Serbian border, but was careful to avoid such mobilization against the Russians. It might be thought that the field marshal should have been satisfied with a crushing defeat of the Serbs. More likely, he was aiming for delayed action on the part of the Russians. The longer it took Russia to mobilize, the greater the chances for a speedy combined German-Austrian attack and ultimate victory over all its "enemies." In any event, the field marshal did not launch his troops against Serbia at once. He considered August 12 (for what reason, we cannot possibly know) a more suitable date for a declaration of war against Serbia.

On July 26, the London foreign office again suggested a four-power discussion of the problem. Paris diplomatically accepted the proposal. Rome was willing to go along with it but rejected the British suggestion that Italy bring pressure on her allies, Germany and Austria, to agree to the conference. Sazonov, in a considerably calmer manner, his fury tempered by friendly talks with both Austrian and German diplomats, suggested that King George V of England mediate the conflict between Belgrade and Vienna, and that the four-power talks be postponed while Russia continued direct talks with Austria-Hungary.

Berlin played a more complicated and devious game. While it endorsed direct talks between the Russians and the Austro-Hungarians, it permitted, perhaps encouraged, noisy, belligerent anti-Serbian and anti-Russian demonstrations in its streets. Moreover, it directly encouraged Austria-Hungary to make its military move. On the twenty-sixth, the Austro-Hungarian ambassador in Berlin, Count Szögyény, was able to wire his government in Vienna, "We are urgently advised to proceed without delay and to place before the world a *fait accompli.*"

On the twenty-seventh, Kaiser Wilhelm II, aboard his imperial yacht, was handed Serbia's reply to the Hapsburg ultimatum. He read it and was rather amazed by its conciliatory, almost sycophantic, tone.

"This is more than we expected! A great moral success for Vienna!" he is reported to have remarked. "Every reason for war drops away. Giesl might have remained quietly in Belgrade. On the strength of this *I* should never have ordered mobilization!"

He hurried off a note to Gottlieb von Jagow, the German secretary for foreign affairs, instructing him to inform the Austrians of his reaction to Serbia's response to the ultimatum. The cause for war, as the kaiser saw it, no longer existed. Vienna should do no more than occupy Belgrade to ensure the execution of Serbia's promises.

Sir Edward Grey of Britain had suggested almost the same procedure for the Hapsburgs that very day; Italy concurred.

But Theobald von Bethmann-Hollweg, the German chancellor, and Gottlieb von Jagow of the German foreign office were not to be denied the war they wanted. Deliberately, they delayed sending the kaiser's message to Heinrich von Tschirschky, the kaiser's ambassador in Vienna. When the message did reach him, it was too late. The Austro-Hungarian Empire had already declared war on Serbia on July 28, 1914, exactly one month after the assassination of the Archduke Franz Ferdinand and his wife in Sarajevo.

Only a few days before the declaration of war, Wilhelm II had sent off a note to his cousin, Czar Nicholas II: "I am exerting my utmost influence to induce Austria to deal honestly and to arrive at a satisfactory understanding with you."

The note was signed, "Your very sincere and devoted friend and cousin, Willy."

Only three hours earlier, Czar Nicholas had sent his cousin Wilhelm a note: "In the name of our old friendship . . . stop your allies from going too far."

This note was signed, simply, "Nicky."

Neither note did anything to stop the rush to the holocaust.

On June 29, Britain warned that it might not remain neutral in the event the war spread on the Continent. Russia was warned by Germany to discontinue its mobilization. "Willy" wrote to "Nicky": "Military measures on the part of Russia which would be looked on as threatening by Austria would precipitate a calamity we both wish to avoid."

Russia would continue its mobilization. The czar had signed two decrees within twenty-four hours after the Hapsburg declaration of war against Belgrade. One decree called for partial mobilization of the Russian armed forces. The second called for a general mobilization as circumstances demanded.

Helmuth von Moltke, chief of staff of the German armies, urged the kaiser not to delay mobilization of the German forces. He also sent a secret note to the German minister in Brussels, a note to be delivered when ordered to the Belgian government. The note was actually an ultimatum demanding that the Belgians permit German troops to march through their country unopposed.

Von Bethmann-Hollweg, meanwhile, approached the British with an impossible proposition: if Britain remained neutral, Germany would give its assurances "that in case of a victorious war in Europe we would not aspire to any territorial increase at France's expense in Europe." He gave Britain a similar promise with respect to Belgium and Holland, if those two countries did not join forces with Germany's enemy.

The British rejected the proposition out of hand.

Winston Churchill, first lord of the British admiralty at the time, ordered the British fleet to proceed to its battle stations and to prepare for action. He was covering the European ports of the English Channel in the event the Germans launched an attack in that area, which was vital to the British defenses. Lord Grey, still hopeful that the peace could be saved, asked both France and Germany to give their assurances that Belgian neutrality, in accordance with the treaty signed by all major European powers, would not be violated. The French gave the assurance requested. Germany declined, suggesting that secret war plans made it impossible for it to commit itself to any such promise. The Germans did not reveal that the "secret war plans" were their own.

British action worried, momentarily, the German chancellor, Theobald von Bethmann-Hollweg; but not Field Marshal Helmuth von Moltke. On July 30, the concerned von Bethmann-Hollweg wired the German ambassador in Vienna: "We stand, in case Austria refuses all mediation, before a conflagration in which England will be against us; Italy and Rumania to all appearances will not go with us, and we two shall be opposed to four great Powers. . . . Under these circumstances we must urgently and impressively suggest to the consideration of the Vienna cabinet, the acceptance of mediation. . . . The responsibility for the consequences that would otherwise follow would be an uncommonly heavy one both for Austria and for us."

General von Moltke, on the other hand, wired Conrad von Hötzendorf on the same day: "Stand firm against Russian mobilization. Austria-Hungary must be preserved. Mobilize at once against Russia. Germany will mobilize."

The general staffs and the commanders in chief of the European armies were beginning to take over the diplomatic maneuvering and action on the Continent.

In France, General Joseph Jacques Joffre, the French

commander in chief, urged Russia to ready itself for a quick attack in the event of war. The Russians were given full assurance of French support, and Britain, in addition to being pressed for military commitment, was urged to begin precautionary defense measures. In the streets of Paris, the citizens of France, undoubtedly abetted by the military, were demonstrating for war, for revenge. "On to Berlin!"

Austria's answer to German General von Moltke's wire was the ordering of immediate mobilization. On the same day, July 30, Russia ordered general mobilization of its armies. On July 31, the next day, Germany proclaimed a "state of danger of war" and sent an ultimatum to Russia threatening a mobilization of the German armed forces "if Russia does not suspend every war measure against Austria-Hungary and ourselves within twelve hours and make a distinct declaration to that effect."

At the same time, the German ambassador in Paris was instructed to deliver an ultimatum to France, part of which was open, part secret. The open segment, to be communicated at once to the French authorities, demanded to know whether France intended to remain neutral in the event of German hostilities against Russia. The secret part (which was not delivered) requested German occupation of the French frontier fortresses as a guarantee of neutrality should there be war between Russia and Germany.

Russia, in reply to the German ultimatum, agreed to stop its military preparations, if the Hapsburgs agreed to respect the sovereignty of Serbia. The reply was not to the satisfaction of the Germans.

The reply of the French to the German ultimatum was the immediate mobilization of the French army.

August 1, 1914, Germany declared war on Russia.

August 1, 1914, the German minister in Brussels presented the Belgians with the pre-prepared ultimatum demanding the free passage of troops through Belgium. Belgium rejected the ultimatum.

August 3, 1914, Germany declared war on France.

August 3, 1914, the Germans began a massive attack against the Belgians.

August 4, 1914, Britain delivered an ultimatum to Germany demanding assurances that the German forces would be withdrawn from Belgian territory. The response to the ultimatum from Berlin was unsatisfactory. At midnight, August 4, 1914, Britain declared war on Germany.

The murders in Sarajevo in late June were all but forgotten. They would be remembered again, after the war, when the diplomats, generals and political observers of every country involved in the holocaust that followed would be involved in trying to fix the blame for the dreadful bloodshed and destruction caused by the war.

Meanwhile, in Sarajevo, Gavrilo Princip, Nedeljko Cabrinovic, Danilo Ilic, and the host of others accused of participation in the June assassinations waited in their jail cells, in chains, for their trials, which were scheduled to begin in the middle of October, in the midst of the bloodiest war Europe had ever experienced.

War

17

THE GERMANS had been preparing for a general European war for years. Specifically, they had been readying themselves for a two-front conflict, against the French and possibly the British in the west, against the Russians in the east. The battle strategy, carefully discussed and constructed by the chiefs of its general staff, beginning with its triumph in the Franco-Prussian War of 1870–71, reached its final definition under Count Alfred von Schleiffen, who headed the general staff of the German armies from 1891 to 1905. The Schleiffen Plan, as it came to be called, specified a holding operation against the Russians, while the main German thrust would move through Belgium, outflank the French defenses and swiftly move on Paris. Once Paris was taken and France defeated, Germany could concentrate on the larger and more cumbersome armies of the Russians.

Keeping to the Schleiffen Plan, despite the unexpectedly brave and tough resistance of the Belgians, the overwhelming German forces encountered little difficulty in their march through that little country and within a month were at the Marne and Meuse Rivers, at Verdun, and within big-gun distance of Paris. But here, under the French generals Joseph Jacques Foch and Joseph Simon Galliens and the British general Sir

John French, the British and French troops held. Whether the Germans could have pushed on and defeated the combined Anglo-French forces is a debatable question; for some inexplicable reason the kaiser ordered his armies to retreat. The German armies moved back to the Aisne River but no farther. They dug themselves in, in French territory, and there they were to stay, in their trenches.

The German push for the English Channel ports was no more successful. It was bogged down in the first battle at Ypres, in which both the British and the Germans suffered heavy losses. Again the Germans dug in. So did the British. For approximately three years there would be little marked movement on the Western Front. It would be dirty, bloody, and costly trench warfare, from Ostend, past Armentières, Donali, Saint Quentin, Rheims, Verdun and Saint Mihiel, to Lunéville, until the arrival of the American Expeditionary Forces in 1918 would break the stalemate.

On the Eastern Front, the Germans were more successful against an ill-trained, ill-equipped Russian force. At Tannenberg, General Paul von Hindenburg virtually annihilated a Russian army, taking some ninety thousand prisoners. The Russian commander, General Alexandr Vasilyevich Samsonon, committed suicide. In East Prussia, in the Battle of the Masurian Lakes, as at Tannenberg, the defeated Russians lost one hundred twenty-five thousand men. Warsaw, which was Russian territory at the time, was taken by the Germans on August 5, 1915. In 1916, the Russians lost one million men in a futile and disastrously executed counteroffensive.

But, as Napoleon had discovered in 1812, Russia is too vast to be conquered by an invader. The defeat of Russia had to be devised by its own people. That would come to pass in 1917. Till then, however, Germany would have to keep its line of troops on its Eastern Front and fight a two-front war.

At sea, there was one great naval battle between the Allies and the Central Powers (Germany and its allies). It was fought sixty miles west of Jutland, the Danish peninsula. Both the British and the Germans (the only belligerents in the battle) suffered heavy losses. Eleven German ships went down into the sea, and some twenty-five hundred men were killed. The British casualties were even greater: fourteen ships lost and about six thousand men dead. It may have been considered an inconclusive test of strength, or even a victory for the Germans. But in truth it was neither. From the end of May 1916, the date of the Battle of Jutland, the German fleet never left port until the end of the war. Its battleships had been completely bottled up. Jutland, however, did not put an end to Germany's war on—or under—the seas. The Germans possessed a powerful corps of submarines, a weapon which they would use to wreak havoc among the Allied merchant marine and disrupt Allied trade and procurement of weapons. It was also to be a principal factor in bringing the United States into the war, and in the eventual defeat of the German Empire.

August 23, 1914, Japan declared that a state of war existed between Japan and Germany.

October 29, 1914, Turkish battleships bombarded Russian Black Sea ports.

On May 23, 1915, Italy, as was not unexpected, tore away from its Triple Alliance with Germany and Austria-Hungary to join the side of the Allies. Less than a month before—April 26, 1915—Italy, Britain, Russia, and France had met in London and signed a secret treaty. The treaty guaranteed the Italians would re-

ceive Trentino, South Tyrol, Trieste, Istria, the Dodec-
anes Islands, and other Austrian-held territory, as well
as some prizes in Africa, with the proviso that Rome
send its armed forces against the Austrian armies
within four weeks of the agreement.

There were other secret agreements among the powers, even as the armies of the Central Powers occupied
Allied territory and seemed to be winning the war.
March 12, 1915, Britain and France agreed to Russia's
annexation of Constantinople, the western coast of the
Bosporus, and the Dardanelles Straits, while Russia as-
sented to Britain's occupation of the so-called neutral
area in Persia.

On April 26, 1916, there was another secret pact
signed by the British, the Russians and the French. This
time Britain was to be granted southern Mesopotamia,
Bagdad, and two ports in Syria. Russia was to be given
Trebizond, Erzerum, Bitlis, Van, and some areas of
southern Kurdistan. France was assigned Syria, western Kurdistan, and the Adana.

Bulgaria, seizing the opportunity to avenge its defeat
by Serbia in the Second Balkan War, joined the Central
Powers on October 2, 1915, in a formal agreement, and
on October 10 sent its troops smashing into Serbian
territory.

Eventually, almost every country in Europe would
become involved, on about a half dozen fronts, but the
war's outcome was to be decided on the Western Front,
where the French army and the greater part of the
British and German forces were bogged down in what
had become a war of attrition. It was a question of
which people of which country could take the greatest
hardships, the greatest losses, for the longest time.

When troops, after a preparatory heavy bombard-
ment by their artillery, left their trenches and went

"over the top" in what was generally a vain attempt to break through enemy lines with their bayonets fixed, they were met by withering machine-gun fire on "no man's land," the bomb-torn area between opposing trenches. Wave on wave they dropped, shouting defiance, each in his own language, wounded, killed. At Ypres, the British lost fifty thousand men. In the Allied drive of the summer of 1916, more than one million Germans, French, and British were wounded or killed; and the offensive, for all the horrible casualties, netted the Allies no more than an insignificant twenty-five hundred square yards. And the trench warfare in the west, with all its bloody horrors, went on.

Rumania joined the Allied forces. So did Portugal. So did Greece. It did not change the picture.

Britain made an attempt to force the Germans to cut their troop strength on the French and Belgian fronts. If the Russians could mount a serious offensive in the east, Berlin would be required to bolster the Austro-Hungarian forces. This would entail the withdrawal of a significant number of regiments from the German-held trenches in the west. Unfortunately, while Russia had the men for such a drive as the British envisioned, it was badly lacking in war matériel. Britain's strategy called for delivering that matériel.

There were two routes the British might take for delivery of arms to the Russians. One was by way of the Baltic. But this route had been cut off by German victories at Tannenberg and the Masurian Lakes. The only other possibility was by fleet, through the Turkish Dardanelles Strait and into the Black Sea. Courageously, but futilely, the British drove for the straits. Unfortunately for the Allies, it proved an abysmally inept campaign. The Turks, assisted by the Germans, held. The British suffered almost two hundred fifteen thousand casualties. The Western Front, for all purposes, continued to remain stationary.

In the second battle of Ypres, against all agreed-upon covenants of war, the Germans introduced the use of poison gas. It gained them a momentary advantage, but that was all. The British came up with a crude gas mask, and the gas, in any case, went with the wind, moving at times into the unprepared German lines as well. Poison-gas warfare did not last very long.

In September 1916, the British gained a momentary advantage, introducing the tank as a battle weapon. But the Allies had not learned how to follow up on the small advantage gained by their tanks, and the Germans recouped their small losses quickly. The opposing battle lines remained relatively fixed.

It had been assumed, at least by the German general staff, that the war would be of short duration, that it would be won by the swift and compelling force of Germany's well-trained, well-organized, strategically employed German armies. By their mathematical calculations, they had figured it would take the superior German forces no more than six weeks to conquer France. Russia, it was reckoned, would then fall of its own slow and inept weight. Britain would then be completely isolated and forced to sue for peace, on German terms. It all looked good on paper. The reality of the situation was something for which they were not prepared.

The British fleet had effectively blockaded all German ports of entry, cutting off much of the raw materials the Germans required for their armaments. Perhaps even more important, the blockade cut sharply into the German import of food and foodstuffs, creating severe shortages in such necessities as bread and meat for the home front. And the news from the battle zones, de-

spite the continuous flow of enthusiastic reports of victory after victory, did nothing to assuage the sufferings
of the German civilian population. There was the growing list of dead and missing in action, and the hospitals
were crowded with the wounded.

Instead of the quick victory they had envisioned, the
German general staff had not succeeded in a single one
of its major objectives. There existed nothing more, on
the critical Western Front, than a balance of power
between the major belligerents. Neither the Central
Powers nor the Allies had what might be recognized as
a distinct advantage in military position; and at home,
the French and British population, no less than the
German, had been forced to tighten their belts and live
with shortages (in Britain even potatoes were rationed)
because of Germany's effective blockade of French and
British ports.

"God is with us," as the British said, or "Gott ist mit
uns," as the Germans said; it seemed, after three years
of the most costly warfare, that neither foe was ready
to recognize defeat, that the war would continue until
all the antagonists dropped their arms out of sheer ex-
haustion or died of starvation.

Even before the hostilities had begun, before the
assassinations in Sarajevo, Woodrow Wilson, president
of the United States, in an effort to ease the tensions in
Europe and to stop what was deemed an inevitable
war, had sent his personal emissary to Paris, to London,
and to Berlin. His aim had been to bring the antagonists
into a series of conferences, to settle by arbitration
whatever differences they had.

When Colonel Edward Mandell House (the *Colonel*
was one of those honorary titles; he was not a military
man) arrived in Germany in the spring of 1914, he was
given the full army-officer treatment, including a display of German derring-do in the air and a special mili-

tary display at Potsdam, as well as a top-brass lunch with the kaiser. He had a long private talk with the kaiser, too, and was impressed by his "charm." But the German monarch showed no enthusiasm for Woodrow Wilson's concept of arbitration. Certainly he would not allow Germany to commit itself to any kind of treaty which demanded a cooling-off period and binding mediation.

"Our strength lies in being prepared for war at a second's notice," he said to Colonel House. "We will not resign that advantage and give our enemies time to prepare."

In Paris, the colonel's next stop, the president of France, Jules Henri Poincaré, was too preoccupied with preparations for a critical visit to St. Petersburg to give much thought or time to House's mission. In London, the British were affable, entertaining, and impressed with the American's ideas and his good will, but the prospect of settling the differences between the European nations by arbitration was as dim as it had ever been.

In the winter of 1915–16, with the big powers locked in their bloody war struggle, Woodrow Wilson sent his personal envoy across the seas again. This time the mission of Colonel House was to attempt to bring the belligerents to a peace table. The mission failed completely.

The Germans would consider no peace proposals which did not include huge indemnities for its war costs and losses, and which did not allow for German occupation (annexation) of Belgium and much, if not all, of Poland.

In London, the British were as affable as always, but the mention of "peace" ruffled their spines. *Peace* had become a pro-German word.

The French were even more difficult. For some completely inexplicable reason, France was of the belief that the American president, Woodrow Wilson, was secretly hoping for a German victory.

Nor were the French or the English less demanding than the Germans with respect to the conditions they expected to be met before they would even begin to consider joining their enemies in talks of peace.

Toward the end of 1916, Woodrow Wilson, a man who would die in his efforts to bring about a world in which peace would be sacred and inviolable, tried once more. This time he asked Berlin, Paris, and London to state their war aims, what it was they wished to attain before they put down their arms and brought to an end the horrible slaughter in Europe.

The intention was to attain a clarification of purpose. If each of the belligerents arrived at a clear understanding in this area, perhaps they would be more willing to sit down in a conference of nations. The conference, or conferences, might well lead to compromise. Compromise was surely the road to peace.

Like the missions of Colonel House, it was a worthy effort. Unfortunately, like the other missions, it would fall on deaf ears and stubborn minds, get nowhere, stop none of the bloodshed, none of the dreadful waste of human energies and human life.

Both the Germans and the Allies sent carefully worded replies to the American president's request, and both were mild in their phrasing, almost conciliatory. Both, too, were not without a touch of hypocrisy.

The responses of the belligerents were aimed not so much at the truth as at gaining the sympathy of the Americans and influencing their attitudes toward the different belligerents and toward the war itself.

The Allies asked that Germany withdraw its armies from all the territories it had taken in its war drive; it also asked for the expropriation of all Turkish territory in Europe, and the reorganization of the Continent with a respect for all nationalities and national aspirations. The Allied note made no mention of the provisions in all the secret treaties they had signed among themselves, nor of the proposed division of territories and spheres of influence, regardless of nationalist aspiration.

The German statement, which was delivered to President Wilson for his personal information only, actually offered to return to France part of the province of Alsace, but it did not budge from its demand for land in Poland and compensation for its war costs; and, this time, the Germans added a demand for land in Africa for colonies.

Obviously there was no give-and-take proposition in the camps of either the Allies or the Central Powers, and the trench warfare and the suffering of the peoples of Europe continued. It would not be until the year 1917 that anything of real significance would alter the pattern of the European War.

In 1917 there were two revolutions in Russia, revolutions which would "shake the world."

In 1917, too, the United States would finally enter the war and significantly affect the balance of power, break the stalemate, and bring the war to its bloody conclusion.

In Russia, a cruel ineptness, a callous indifference on the part of the czarist regime to the suffering of its people and its tremendous losses of life in the battlefields, was responsible for riots, mutinies, and eventually rebellion in Petrograd (renamed from St. Petersburg during the war). The first revolution, led by the socialists, forced the abdication of the Romanov, Czar Nicholas II. A provisional republican government, with

Alexander Kerensky as minister of war, kept the Russian armies in the field against the German and Austro-Hungarian forces; but not for long. More riots, more mutinies followed, and, on November 10, 1917, the Bolsheviks, led by Nikolai Lenin and Leon Trotsky, took over. The second Russian revolution pulled the Russian troops out of the field and brought them home, taking Russia out of the war.

The civil wars which followed this second revolution were undoubtedly a factor in the treaty which the Bolsheviks signed at Brest-Litovsk, March 3, 1918. The Russians ceded much to the German conquerors (all of which it was eventually to regain). But it was more than land that the Germans had won. Russia was knocked out of the war. The German armies, except for a minor force to police its victory in the east, could be concentrated on one front—the Western Front.

The advantage this gave the Central Powers was enormous, except for one factor; by this time the United States of America was landing the first detachments of its Expeditionary Forces in France.

It was Germany's excellent and efficient submarine warfare, a warfare the United States would not and could not countenance, which was largely responsible for bringing the Americans across the Atlantic. It was this devastating submarine warfare of the Germans which brought an armed force three thousand miles across an ocean to deliver a humiliating defeat to the German Empire.

America Decided

18

ON JUNE 29, 1914, the *New York Times* devoted a front-page story to the assassination of Archduke Franz Ferdinand of Austria-Hungary and his wife. It also printed an interview with the brilliant professor of electromechanics at Columbia University, Michael Pupin. Pupin, who was also the top officer of the nine-thousand-member Americans of Serbian Descent organization, found reason for the assassination in the Hapsburg persecution of the Serbs living in the Austrian provinces of Bosnia and Hercegovina. Pupin and his organization, incidentally, were under the constant and careful surveillance of the Hapsburg intelligence service working secretly in the United States, and had been accused of fostering and abetting would-be political murderers.

There was an interview, too, in the *New York Times* of that date with the well-known anarchist Alexander Berkman. Berkman, according to the news item, called the assassination "a plot of the anarchists and revolutionaries." Later, he was to write that the "Serbian patriot" Gavrilo Princip "had never heard of anarchism."

A few desultory follow-up articles and an almost negligent report of the trials which followed was all that appeared in America's leading newspaper. Like the overwhelming majority of citizens in America, the *New*

York Times treated the assassinations in Sarajevo as part of the continuing petty disturbances in the Balkans. With the outbreak of the war that engulfed Europe, Sarajevo and the assassinations disappeared from both the mind and the press of America.

After a quick and short-lived panic on Wall Street— stocks plummeting because Europeans were selling their American holdings to stock up on gold, with its price soaring—there was a burst of activity in the mills, in the mines, and in agriculture, which sent the economy of the United States on a steep upward flight. In the very first month of the European war, Charles M. Schwab, president of the Bethlehem Steel Corporation, came home from the Continent with a British order for shells and other war matériel that broke all records, the largest such order in the history of the world. A few weeks later it was the DuPonts who were deluged with an order for approximately five hundred million dollars worth of gunpowder. Again, it was an order from Britain, and gunpowder was selling at a price which had jumped almost one hundred percent in the first four weeks of the European hostilities. On August 4, 1914, Woodrow Wilson had proclaimed the United States neutral in the conflict, but in the summer and fall of that year millions of Americans prospered in jobs that provided the Allies with everything from weapons of war to ordinary mules.

There was nothing in American policies or politics to prevent the Germans from placing similar orders in the United States, procuring the same goods the British were getting, by the hundreds of tons, if they had the money or the credit. But Britain controlled the seas; its ships stopped every vessel that came within its range, no matter what flag it flew. If the boat was headed for a German port, or even a neutral port, its cargo was carefully examined for contraband; and contraband, to the British, meant anything that might contribute to the enemy war effort, everything from the raw materials for ammunition to wheat, meat, or anything else the Germans could eat. One of the main purposes of the British naval blockade was to attack the enemy's morale by starving its civilian population, and precious little foodstuffs got through to the German people. An offending ship, a ship carrying what the British labeled contraband, was escorted to an Allied port and quickly divested of cargo.

The United States protested these actions on the part of Britain. We had gone to war with the British in 1812 to keep the seas free, but this time our protests were mild, and mildly answered; and the incidents, even as they continued, were generally forgotten. In truth, our government, despite its declaration of neutrality, had been sympathetic to the Allied cause from the begin-ning. In 1915 Woodrow Wilson lifted the ban he had placed on commercial loans to the warring nations and sanctioned a five-hundred-million-dollar Anglo-French bond issue. This was the first of many such issues. The Germans, who were free to take advantage of the lifting of the ban, also managed to raise some money in the United States. It was a pittance, however, compared to the huge sums of money Americans invested in the British and the French.

Actually, governmental policies and the activities of the monied interests did not accurately reflect the attitudes of the American people toward the different belligerents and toward the war itself. While a proportionately large segment of the American population was of English and Scotch descent (Woodrow Wilson himself was of Scotch Presbyterian stock), there was by 1914 a great mingling of peoples whose fathers and grandfathers had come from almost every country in Europe. In that year, fully one-third of the people in the United States were foreign born. Their foreign heritages and biases were still much alive, and many of them, in 1914, were ardently hoping for a German victory.

It would be more correct to say they were anti-British or anti-Russian rather than pro-German—although in the large cities, and particularly in the Midwest, there was a considerable number of citizens of German descent. It was in the large cities, too, especially on the East Coast, that the Irish had settled, and no group of people was more anti-British than the Irish, who brought their memories and experience of the "Irish troubles" with them. Nor were there any who were more anti-Russian than the American Jews, who had fled persecution (and massacres) in Russia and Poland.

Above and beyond all these deep passions, however, was a stronger sentiment among all the peoples of the United States: Keep us out of Europe. Keep us out of the war. We don't want our young men to die in Europe, for Europe.

And this was exactly in line with German policy. It was the specifically assigned task of the German ambassador in Washington, Johann-Heinrich von Bernstorff, to keep the United States out of the conflict. Berlin knew well enough that if America entered the war, it would be on the side of the Allies, not the Central Powers.

But German war policy clashed with its diplomacy. Particularly, it was the submarine warfare of the Germans which eventually destroyed the purpose of their ambassador. The German U-boats did a devastatingly effective job for the German war machine, but they also eventually torpedoed whatever good relations existed between Germany and the United States.

On March 15, 1915, a U-boat sank a British passenger vessel, the *Falaba*. One American lost his life in the sinking. On April 28, an American ship, the *Cushing*, was the recipient of German gunfire. On May 1, the *Gunflight*, an American vessel, was torpedoed, and two more Americans lost their lives. It was the sinking of the *Lusitania*, however, on May 7, 1915, which created irreparable damage to any possible German-American amity.

The *Lusitania*, sailing toward the port of Liverpool, England, was hit by a single torpedo just off the Irish coast. It sank beneath the waters in no more than eighteen minutes. One thousand one hundred ninety-eight passengers and members of the ship's crew were killed. Of that number, 139 were Americans, most of them women and children.

The reaction in the United States was an instant angry indignation, an almost unbelieving horror. All at once the Germans were everything the British propaganda machines had said they were: brutal, bestial "Huns." The burning of the cities of Dinant and Louvain by the Germans, the indiscriminate shooting of masses of innocent hostages, a host of other barbarous, villainous, uncivilized actions were recalled; and the pressure which previously had been relatively slight, to enter the war as an open belligerent against Germany, became marked and vociferous. Even among the more pacifistic of the pacifists it became obvious that the United States could not stay out of the conflict forever.

The young blood—college graduates, writers, painters, the literati—could not wait. They jumped the gun. Eager to retaliate for German brutalities (real or propaganda-inspired), or just out of the spirit of adventure, they enlisted by droves in the British, the Canadian, and the French forces. They joined the French Foreign Legion. They organized a volunteer air force, the *Escadrille Americaine,* later renamed the *Lafayette Escadrille,* in honor of the Marquis de Lafayette, the young French nobleman who had come to America and volunteered his services in the cause of its 1776 revolution.

There were other ways to aid the Allied cause. Young Americans, many of whom were to become prominent in the theatre, in fiction, in poetry, in the other arts, joined up with the Canadian Royal Air Force, drove transport trucks in France and Belgium, organized the American Volunteer Ambulance Corps. Among them were such distinguished names as John Dos Passos, Ernest Hemingway, William Faulkner, Louis Bromfield, E. E. Cummings, Harry Crosby, and William Seabrook. Many others never returned to the United States.

America was still officially neutral. It was a neutrality which became more and more difficult to explain, or to keep.

President Woodrow Wilson sent a sharp note of protest to the Germans following their sinking of the *Lusitania,* but Berlin was not inclined to take the protest seriously. As important a figure in the United States government as secretary of state William Jennings Bryan, reading the report that the *Lusitania* had been carrying 4,200 cases of cartridges and 1,259 cases of shells when it went down in the Irish Sea accused Britain of "using our citizens to protect her ammunition."

Germany's reply to the American protest was entirely unsatisfactory to Woodrow Wilson, and he let Berlin know it. The Germans became conciliatory. They promised not to sink ships without prior warning, and to safeguard the lives of noncombatants on these ships. It was a promise which would not be kept very long. But America remained officially neutral, and, in 1916, Woodrow Wilson began his second term as president of the United States, re-elected with the slogan, "He kept us out of the war."

That, too—keeping America out of the war—would not last.

On the twenty-fourth of March, 1916, the Germans torpedoed the British steamer *Sussex*, without warning and without safeguard for noncombatants, as it had pledged. Eighty passengers were killed or wounded. There had been twenty-five Americans aboard the *Sussex*. Four of them were injured.

The lull in tensions between Germany and the United States was over. President Wilson sent his sharpest note to Berlin.

"Unless the Imperial Government should now declare its intention to abandon its present practices of submarine warfare . . . the United States can have no choice but to sever relations with the German Empire."

Again Berlin promised a more humanitarian approach in its U-boat strikes, and kept its promise for a while; but only for a relatively short while.

On January 9, 1917, while Colonel House was in Europe on yet another of Woodrow Wilson's peace missions, Kaiser Wilhelm II sent a secret message to his fleet.

"I order that unrestricted submarine war be launched with the greatest vigor on the first of February.

"You will immediately take all necessary steps, taking care however that this intention shall not prematurely come to the knowledge of the enemy and neutral powers."

The new attacks, to be most effective, were to come as a complete surprise to the allies and to the United States.

To make matters even worse, Arthur Zimmerman, the new and bellicose German secretary for foreign affairs, sent a coded message to Germany's minister in Mexico, Heinrich von Eckhardt, the message to be transmitted secretly to Venustiano Carranza, president of Mexico.

"We propose alliance to Mexico upon the following basis: To make war together; make peace together; generous financial support; and agreement on our part that Mexico shall reconquer . . . Texas, New Mexico, Arizona . . ."

The possibility of getting Japan to join the Central Powers, with Mexican assistance, was also proposed in the coded message.

The communication—which Germany was later to admit, almost boastfully, was genuine, not a forgery—was intercepted by British intelligence, decoded, and eventually sent on to Washington.

This overt act of belligerence, along with the kaiser's order to renew unrestricted submarine warfare on foe and neutral alike, could lead to only one decision on the part of the United States. On February 3, 1917, Count Johann-Heinrich von Bernstorff, the German ambassador, was asked to leave Washington. The United States broke off all diplomatic relations with Germany.

The next steps were inevitable. President Wilson called for a joint session of Congress, April 2, 1917. He called for a declaration of war against the German Empire.

"The world," he declared, "must be made safe for democracy."

On April 6, 1917, after a considerably heated debate

—for there was still much anti-British and anti-war sentiment in Congress—the House and Senate voted the declaration for which President Wilson had asked. The United States, at last, was in the conflict, at war with the Central Powers.

With the Russians out of the war, the Germans mounted a huge offensive on the Western Front, intending to crush the Allies before the American troops could arrive in sufficient force to change the tide of battle. It was the last German offensive of the war.

On the last days of May 1918, the Americans were at Chateau-Thierry in their first significant action. They held the German tide. Early in June, the Americans counterattacked and took the Belleau Wood. They were good soldiers. In July and August, in the second battle of the Marne, they helped stop the Germans short of Paris. The German offensive was blunted; it was time for the Allied forces to bring all their might to bear on an attack to drive the enemy out of France, out of Belgium, to end the war.

The Americans, under General John Joseph "Black Jack" Pershing, the British, under Field Marshal Sir Douglas Haig, and the rest of the Allied forces—all under the single command of Supreme Allied Commander Ferdinand Foch—moved as a unit against the common enemy. They would not be stopped.

The end came quickly.

On September 30, 1918, the Bulgarians surrendered unconditionally.

October 30, 1918, Turkey gave up the battle.

On November 4, 1918, following their defeat at the hands of the Italians at Vittorio Veneto, the Hapsburgs surrendered. The Austro-Hungarian Empire fell apart as its different national groups rebelled and declared themselves independent republics.

November 9, Kaiser Wilhelm II abdicated and, on the tenth, fled to Holland for sanctuary.

November 11, at Compiègne, the new German chancellor, Maximilian, Prince of Baden, accepted the fourteen-point program Woodrow Wilson had proffered as a basis for peace negotiations. Germany was no longer an empire. Revolution, as in so many other areas of Europe, had replaced a monarchy with a republic. The stability and history of those republics is another story.

Wilson's fourteen points were well in line with his desire "to save the world for democracy." They called for open covenants; freedom of the seas in war and in peace; removal of economic barriers between all nations, as far as possible; the reduction of armaments; adjustment of colonial claims; the evacuation and restoration of Russia's territory; preservation of Belgian sovereignty; settlement of the Alsace-Lorraine question; redrawing of Italian frontiers according to national population; the dividing of Austria-Hungary to conform to its nationalities; the redrawing of Balkan boundaries to conform to the different nationalities of the area; Turkish control of its own people only, and freedom of navigation through the Dardanelles Straits; the establishment of a free and independent Poland with access to the sea; and a general association of nations under specific covenants.

The last of the fourteen points referred to Wilson's dream of a League of Nations. It was his inability to get the United States to become a member of such a league which ultimately destroyed him, as a politician, as a diplomat, as a man.

Twenty-two million men, women, and children were killed in the bloody war. Twenty-one million were wounded. The French lost 1,385,000 men, the British 908,000 men, the Italians 650,000 men. Russian losses were a staggering 4,000,000. The United States put 1,390,000 men into battle service. About 50,000 of them never came home.

Germany was forced to accept the guilt for the war, and for the frightful carnage, when it signed its peace treaty with the Allies. Later it would repudiate this responsibility. Certainly all the European powers, and perhaps the United States as well, shared this horrendous guilt in one way or another.

Strangely enough—or perhaps not so strangely— there was little mention of the conspirators who had succeeded in assassinating the archduke of Austria and his wife in Sarajevo, the cruel incident which had presented the European powers with at least the excuse for taking those big steps toward the Armageddon of 1914–18.

Those conspirators who had been apprehended— Gavrilo Princip, Nedeljko Cabrinovic, Danilo Ilic, and their known associates—had been tried by Austrian judges and had paid in one way or another for what they had deemed a patriotic act. Dragutin Dimitrijevic, the Apis of the Black Hand, was tried by his own people and, guilty or innocent, his punishment was final.

Trials and Judgment   19

THERE had been some debate among the Austro-Hungarians as to the date to be set for the trials of the Sarajevo assassins. Leon von Bilinski, the Hapsburg minister of finance, who was also responsible for the administration of Bosnia-Hercegovina, thought it might be postponed till after the end of the war that had begun at the end of July 1914. General Oskar Potiorek, the Austrian governor of Bosnia, was of a like mind. Count Leopold von Berchtold, the Austro-Hungarian foreign minister, however, wanted the trial of the accused to begin at once. He also urged that the judges be aware of the international implications in their sentences of the guilty. Undoubtedly he was eager to fix the responsibility for the outbreak of the European holocaust on the Serbs. The responsibility for starting the war was a moral question. It was a question which occupied the serious attention of all the belligerents involved. It is a question which remains, to this day, a serious one for diplomats, students, and historians.

Following a long investigation, the indictments were delivered to the accused on September 28, 1914, exactly three months after the assassinations had taken place. The trials of the accused began exactly two weeks later, at a courthouse in Sarajevo, on October 12, 1914.

There were twenty-five defendents. Heading the list was Gavrilo Princip, whose gun had killed Archduke Franz Ferdinand and the Duchess of Hohenberg; Nedeljko Cabrinovic, who had thrown the bomb at the royal couple; and Trifko Grabez. These three had plotted the assassination, as they testified at their trial, or had been recruited for it in Belgrade. There was Danilo Ilic who had organized an additional team of assassins in Sarajevo, and his two recruits, Vaso Cubrilovic and Cvetko Popovic; the third member of that team, Mehmed Mehmedbasic, could not be found and was never arrested by the Hapsburg officials. Lazar Djukic was another defendant; he had recruited Vaso Cubrilovic for Danilo Ilic. There were the schoolteacher, Veljko Cubrilovic; Misko Jovanovic, the merchant from Tuzla; and the several peasants who had helped transport the assassins and their arsenal from Belgrade to Sarajevo. Four students, accused of prior knowledge of the assassination plot and failure to transmit that knowledge to the police, were also among the accused. Finally, there were Ivo Kranjcevic, Franjo and Angela Sadilo, and Mrs. Sadilo's father, all charged with concealing the weapons of Vaso Cubrilovic after the assassination.

The trial itself, with three judges presiding (there was no jury), was not without an occasional emotional moment. For the most part, however, it provided nothing of a spectacular nature. Gavrilo Princip and his comrades were generally well composed, calm and deliberate. They utilized every opportunity offered them, every crack in the prosecutor's attack, to wallow in polemics on everything from religion to the philosophy of rebellion. They were particularly quick to voice their antagonism toward the Hapsburgs, Franz Ferdinand in particular; and they were aggressive, defining their Slav nationalist credo.

No matter how cleverly the prosecution attempted to get the assassins to reveal a link with the Serbian government, to pin the crime on Serbia, the young assassins held firmly to their original statements. The plot was theirs. The assassination was planned and executed without the advice or counsel of anyone else.

They defended the merchant, the schoolteacher, and the peasants who had been involved as best they could.

"I threatened him," said Trifko Grabez of one of them, "not to tell anyone we had come near his place. . . . 'You will be punished,' I told him, 'by people who are stronger than any soldiers and policemen, and who will kill all the men in your family.' "

This was the line the conspirators took. They also testified that neither peasants nor anyone else knew why they were moving into Sarajevo, and certainly nothing at all of the assassination plot.

The assassins also managed to confuse the situation for the judges on occasion, introducing what was certainly extraneous material. They said that Milan Ciganovic, who had completely disappeared from sight, was a Freemason. This led to considerable investigation into possible Freemason links in the assassination plot, since the archduke himself had once remarked he had been marked for assassination by that anti-Jesuit order. And the assassins cleverly embroidered story and character until one judge was finally forced to ask whether the accused were not creating fables.

If it was the intention of the assassins to conceal the role of Colonel Dragutin Dimitrijevic (Apis) and the Black Hand, they succeeded completely. Neither Apis nor the Black Hand was mentioned throughout the whole period of the trial. Why the judges made no attempt to inquire into this area, considering that they must have had some knowledge of the secret organization, is strangely mystifying. If they had been able to establish some relationship between the Black Hand and the political murders in Sarajevo, there would have been no doubt of Serbia's implication in the crime, and the Hapsburgs would have had what they wanted: the opportunity to lay the blame for the war on Belgrade.

Perhaps, after all, there was no such relationship. Perhaps it was true, as the assassins persistently maintained—even after the trials—that the assassination was entirely the result of the thinking, planning, and action of Gavrilo Princip and his immediate comrades. However, this does not seem too likely. However amateurish the preparations and however clumsy the execution, the history of the Black Hand and particularly the history of its leader, Dimitrijevic, would indicate too strongly that the mind and the intention of that secret terrorist society were the impetus for the entire plot.

Cabrinovic had pleaded guilty to "the crime of Archduke Franz Ferdinand's assassination" on the opening day of the trials in Sarajevo.

Grabez had pleaded guilty to the attempt to assassinate the archduke.

Gavrilo Princip had pleaded not guilty. "I am not a criminal," he said. "I meant to do a good deed."

A little sadly, Nedjo Kerovic, one of the peasants, admitted, "It is possible that I am a little guilty."

This was the plea which most of the peasants on trial made on their own.

On October 22, 1914—after ten days of testimony, dialogue, and cross-examination—the prosecuting attorney, Franjo Svara, summed up his case against the defendants. He accused Serbia of inspiring and arranging the assassinations. He accused twenty-two of the defendants of treason. Treason was a crime which demanded the death sentence, except when the guilty was not of age, not twenty-one years old. He asked for the acquittal of only three—Franjo and Angela Sadilo, and Mrs. Sadilo's father, the people in whose house Cubrilovic had managed to conceal his weapons.

The lawyers for the defendants were ardent, clever, even brilliant. Their clients (they claimed) were the tools of forces beyond the borders of Bosnia. Peasants do not understand the meaning of assassination. Milovic was a smuggler, perhaps, but not a traitor. Cubrilovic was no more than a child. Cabrinovic came from an unhappy home. All had been poisoned by Serbian propaganda. One attorney, Dr. Rudolf Zistler, claimed that none of the defendants was guilty of treason since Bosnia-Hercegovina was not actually part of the Austro-Hungarian Empire. The Hapsburg parliament, he argued, had failed to ratify the annexation of the provinces; therefore Bosnia was not officially Austrian; therefore Bosnians could not be tried under Austrian law.

It was all very clever and dramatic, but the arguments of the attorneys did nothing to sway the final decision of the judges one iota.

The summations over, the prisoners were asked to stand if they regretted the assassination.

They all rose, but one. Gavrilo Princip remained seated.

The defendants were told to take their seats. When one of the judges inquired why he had not stood with the others, Princip calmly announced that he was "sorry for the children who had lost their father and mother." He had not meant to kill the duchess. He had aimed to kill General Oskar Potiorek. He did not regret at all killing the archduke. He had meant to kill him.

Nedeljko Cabrinovic, who would never allow Princip's leadership go without being challenged, who would never allow Princip to play the sole martyr, jumped out of his seat again and shouted, "I do not feel sorry, either!"

The trial came to an end quickly. It had lasted twelve days. Two days later, on October 25, 1914, the judges announced their verdicts.

Gavrilo Princip was found guilty of treason and murder. According to church records, he had been born on either June 13 or July 13, 1894; if the correct date were June 13, he would have been eligible for the death sentence. But the judges, in an unexpected moment of leniency, granted that his birthday was July 13, which meant he had been under twenty years of age at the time of the assassination and therefore exempt, under Austrian law of the time, from execution for whatever crime he may have committed. Accordingly, Princip was sentenced to twenty years of hard labor; he was also sentenced to spend one day a month and each June 28 —the anniversary of the assassination—in solitary confinement, on a hard bed in a darkened cell, with no food and no water.

Nedeljko Cabrinovic and Trifko Grabez, his two comrades from Belgrade, received the same harsh sentence. Neither was of age to be sentenced to death for their guilt.

Danilo Ilic, the schoolteacher Veljko Cubrilovic, and the merchant Misko Jovanovic were less fortunate. They had passed their twentieth birthdays and were sentenced to be hanged. So were Nedjo Kerovic and Jakov Milovic, two of the peasants; but an appeal to a higher court commuted their sentences. Milovic was condemned to life imprisonment, Kerovic to a term of twenty years in jail.

Vaso Cubrilovic was given a sixteen-year prison term, Cvetko Popovic thirteen years, Lazar Djukic ten. Ivo Kranjcevic got ten years, his only crimes having been an attempt to conceal Cabrinovic's bomb and gun and failure to inform the proper authorities. Cvijan Stjepanovic got seven years for not informing the police of what he knew about the assassination plot. Branco Zagorac and Marko Perin received sentences of three years each, for the same "crime."

All others were released. It is easy enough to condemn certain of the sentences passed on the accused, and certainly several of the judgments were particularly harsh. But Austria was at war, and feelings of a country during a war run high. Danilo Ilic had had a mixed viewpoint on the assassination and had tried to stop it. Misko Jovanovic, a Slav patriot, nevertheless should have opposed the assassination on principle if he was aware of its potential victims. Veljko Cubrilovic was certainly opposed to assassination as a political weapon. Yet these were the only ones sentenced to pay with their lives for their roles in the political murder. On February 3, 1915, between nine and ten in the morning, they were hanged in the prison courtyard.

Marko Perin, who was not yet seventeen years old, died in prison before the end of 1914. Nedeljko Cabrinovic was dead in prison before he reached his twenty-second birthday, succumbing to hunger, cold, and the horrors of solitary confinement. Nedjo Kerovic and his father Mitar died of tuberculosis and malnutrition. Jakov Milovic was dead in prison by April 1916, and Trifko Grabez in the winter of the same year. Lazar Djukic went insane from hunger and cold and died in the spring of 1917.

Gavrilo Princip was the last of the Bosnian assassins to die in prison. Tuberculosis had sapped his strength. He had lost an arm to tuberculosis of the bones and had been in and out of the prison hospital. He died in the prison in Theresinstadt, Bohemia, on April 28, 1918.

Of the members of the Black Hand involved in the Sarajevo assassinations, Vojin Takosic died of wounds he received fighting against the Austrian army in the Serbian retreat of December 18, 1915. Milan Ciganovic escaped to the United States, probably with the aid of Nikola Pasic, in 1917. He returned to his native Serbia in 1919, where he lived to die of natural causes in 1927.

The story of Colonel Dragutin Dimitrijevic had a more tragic turn.

In the summer of 1915, he was relieved of his post as chief of intelligence for the general staff of the Serbian army. Alexander, the prince regent of Serbia at the time, was certain that Dimitrijevic was plotting to assassinate him.

On December 15, 1916, Alexander had the colonel arrested. The charges were that Dimitrijevic was not only planning the murder of the prince regent, and Nikola Pasic as well, but was also plotting a mutiny in the army so that he could lead a rebellious Serbian army into the ranks of the enemy Central Powers.

Along with Dimitrijevic, the elusive Mehmed Mehmedbasic, Major Ljubomir Vulovic of the Black Hand executive committee, and Rade Malobabic, the mysterious figure who had appeared in Sarajevo on the eve of the assassinations, were also arrested by the Serbian police. Whether the arrests were the result of Pasic's final efforts to break the power of the Black Hand, or a result of Alexander's fear that Dragutin Dimitrijevic was becoming too powerful a man in the Serbian army —and a threat to his regency—are moot questions. We

do know that, as far as it can be discerned, the colonel
had no secret dealings with either the Germans or the
Austrians during the war. We know, too, that the alleged assassination plot aimed at the regent and at Pasic
was a trumped-up charge. Though Malobabic, probably
after he was subjected to torture by the police, accused
Dimitrijevic of planning the murders, Mehembasic,
who was similarly tortured, denied the existence of
such a plot and declared that the colonel was completely innocent of the charge.

Whatever the case, on April 2, 1917, in Salonika,
Dragutin Dimitrijevic found himself fighting for his life
in what was to prove pretty much a kangaroo court; the
judges who tried him were, for the most part, his old
enemies.

Milan Ciganovic, an old comrade, the man who had
armed the Sarajevo assassins, was brought in to testify
against the Black Hand leader. Ciganovic had been the
informer Pasic had planted in the secret organization.
This probably explained his escape from the authorities
after the 1914 assassinations, while Vojin Tankosic had
been arrested. His testimony against Dimitrijevic was
probably bought by Pasic in exchange for the free trip
Ciganovic was able to take in 1917 out of war-torn
Serbia to the United States.

Djuro Sarac, Vojin Tankosic's old comrade—the man
reportedly sent to Sarajevo to stop the assassination of
the archduke—was another of those formerly associated with the Black Hand to testify against Dimitrijevic.

There were eighty witnesses in all brought in by the
prosecution to condemn the colonel, but the testimony
was flimsy and often obviously fraudulent. Some new
tactic to pin guilt on Dimitrijevic was necessary, and his
enemies found it. One way or another, the colonel was

given to understand that if he confessed to instigating and planning the Sarajevo assassinations, the charges against him might be dropped. Apis, the colonel, bit the bait offered him and on April 11, 1917, he delivered a written confession of his role in the murder of Archduke Franz Ferdinand.

The confession read, in part, "I engaged Malobabic to organize the assassination. . . . I made up my mind on this only when assured that Russia would not leave us without protection if we were attacked by Austria. . . . Malobabic executed my orders, organized and performed the assassination. . . ."

The confession, of course, did not help Dimitrijevic's cause. Nothing could help it. Alexander, and perhaps Pasic also, was determined to get rid of Dimitrijevic for good. On May 23, 1917, the rigged court found Dragutin Dimitrijevic guilty as charged, and he was condemned to death.

Both the British and the Russians urged Alexander to revoke the sentence passed on the colonel. The urging fell on deaf ears. Dimitrijevic, Vulovic, and Malobabic were removed from their jail cells the night of June 25, 1917. They were driven, in closed cars, out of Salonika, where they had been held prisoner, to a lonely spot which had already been prepared for their execution.

The three men were stood up in front of a freshly dug ditch, which was to be their common grave, and, at 4:47 in the morning, June 26, 1917, they died, blindfolded, before a firing squad.

Colonel Dragutin Dimitrijevic's last words were a shout: "Long live Serbia! Long live Yugoslavia!"

*　　*　　*

The Lateiner Bridge in Sarajevo has been renamed Princip Bridge. Princip's footprints are pressed in the pavement in front of the delicatessen shop, marking the spot on which he stood when he killed the Archduke Franz Ferdinand and his wife Sophie. There is also a black marble plaque over the door of the shop. It reads: On this historic spot, Gavrilo Princip initiated freedom on St. Vitus's Day, June 28, 1914.

Mehmed Mehmedbasic was given a sentence of fifteen years for his part in the alleged plot to assassinate Alexander and Pasic. He was released at the end of World War 1.

In 1953, thirty-six years after Dragutin Dimitrijevic's execution, the supreme court of the Federal People's Republic of Yugoslavia retried his case and the cases of those who had been defendants with him. They were all found innocent.

But there are no plaques to the memory of the colonel who organized and led the Black Hand. Yugoslavia, today, prefers to believe that it was not an army cabal, but a young and dedicated revolutionary, a martyr to the Serbian cause, the twenty-year-old, tubercular Gavrilo Princip who, together with his devoted Bosnian comrades, planned and carried out the assassination of the heir to the throne of Austria-Hungary and struck the first blow for the freedom and the unification of the south Slavs—the people of Yugoslavia.

DATE DUE			
MAY 3			